A TASTE OF THE COUNTRY

Editor: Jean Van Dyke
Food Editor: Grace Howaniec
Art Director: Jim Sibilski
Art Associates: Cindy Domin, Gail Engeldahl
Production: Loretta Caughey
Food Photography: Mike Huibregtse

International Standard Book Number: 0-89821-086-0
Library of Congress Catalog Card Number: 88-61945
© 1988, Reiman Associates Inc.,
5400 S. 60th St., Greendale, WI 53129.
Printed in U.S.A.

TO ORDER additional copies of *A Taste of the Country* send $9.98 each plus $3.00
postage and handling to: Country Store, Code **#3018**, Box 572, Milwaukee, WI 53201.

PICTURE THIS: You've just spent a few hours in the brisk outdoors...you're chilled and hungry ...and you head for the house. You open the door, and the delicious aroma of hearty, home-style soup wafts your way.

The kettle you put on the stove earlier is simmering, and—if it's filled with one of the soups shown below—you and your family are in for a real *treat*.

These aren't just light broths that you serve before a meal...

these soups *are* a meal! Served with some steaming muffins or with thick slices of homemade bread, these soups are filling enough to satisfy a woodcutter.

Try one or more of these country classics in *your* kitchen.

HEARTY, HOME-STYLE SOUPS.
Clockwise from lower left: Cream of
Broccoli and Cheese Soup (Pg. 11);
Fish and Cheese Chowder (Pg. 11);
Wintery Day Bean Soup (Pg. 11);
Cheddar Chowder (Pg. 12); Czecho-
slovakian Cabbage Soup (Pg. 12);
Cheese and Potato Wild Rice Soup
(Pg. 12); Grandma's Chicken and
Dumpling Soup (Pg. 11); Upstate
Minestrone Soup (Pg. 11).

EVERYONE loves muffins! And why not? They're easy to make... they add a fresh-baked touch to any meal... and somehow remind us of marvelous meals from kitchens past.

With no pun intended, muffins are hot these days. Everyone's baking them! No longer hum-drum little hand-warmers with ho-hum ingredients, muffins have spiffed up their act and gone a bit glamorous.

Break open today's muffins and you're apt to find shreds of carrot, a hint of maple, chunks of apple or crunchy poppy seed... all mingled tastefully with old-fashioned oats, wheat flour and bran.

You will if you bake and break one of these shown here. Muffins aren't just muffins anymore. They are better... and better for you.

MARVELOUS MUFFINS. Counterclockwise, from right: Maple Bran Muffins (Pg. 12); Oatmeal Apple Raisin Muffins (Pg. 13); Poppy Seed Muffins (Pg. 13); and Carrot Bran Muffins (Pg. 13).

Meals in Minutes

EVERY busy cook is constantly on the lookout for nutritional meals such as this. It's satisfying, delicious and—best of all—ready to eat in less than 30 minutes, including the colorful stir-fry main dish, crunchy lettuce salad with sesame seed dressing and dessert!

STIR FRY BEEF AND BROCCOLI

- 1 pound beef tenderloin, cut in 1/2-inch cubes
- 2 to 3 tablespoons vegetable oil (more if necessary)
- 1/2 cup onion, diced
- 1 pound fresh broccoli, cut in flowerettes
- 1/2 cup chicken broth
- 2 tablespoons soy sauce (or lite soy)
- 1 teaspoon cornstarch
- 4 medium fresh tomatoes, cut in wedges

Brown tenderloin cubes in hot oil in wok or skillet on all sides; remove. Drain on paper towel. Cook onion in oil until tender; remove. Add to beef. Set aside. Add broccoli (along with more oil if necessary). Stir-fry until broccoli is partially tender. Combine broth, soy sauce and cornstarch in small bowl. Add reserved beef and onions to broccoli; pour broth mixture over all. Stir to mix. Lower heat to simmer; simmer 5 minutes, covered. Add tomato wedges; gently mix with other ingredients. Cook until tomatoes are just heated through. Serve on a bed of rice. **Yield:** 4 servings.

BOSTON LETTUCE SALAD WITH SESAME DRESSING

- 1 large head Boston lettuce, rinsed, drained and chilled

VINAIGRETTE DRESSING:
- 3 tablespoons vegetable oil
- 1 tablespoon white vinegar

Recipes from Grace Howaniec, Waukesha, Wisconsin.

- 1/4 teaspoon Dijon mustard
- 1/4 teaspoon salt
- Fresh ground pepper
- 3 tablespoons toasted sesame seeds

Arrange lettuce on individual salad plates. Combine oil, vinegar, mustard, salt and pepper; mix well. Toast sesame seeds in 350° oven in flat pan for 10-12 minutes or until golden. Immediately before serving, drizzle dressing over lettuce; top with sesame seeds. **Yield:** 4 servings.

CHOCOLATE-GLAZED ORANGE CUPS

- 1 quart orange sherbet
- 1/4 cup butter OR margarine
- 1 cup real semi-sweet chocolate chips
- Few drops orange extract OR 1 teaspoon orange liqueur
- 1/4 teaspoon grated orange zest

Thirty minutes before mealtime, form sherbet with round ice cream scoop. Place on plates in freezer. Microwave butter/margarine on HIGH 20-25 seconds in 2-cup glass measure. Add chocolate chips to butter/margarine and microwave on HIGH for 30-45 seconds, stirring once. Add orange extract/liqueur and orange zest; stir to blend. Remove sherbet from freezer; spoon chocolate glaze over sherbet. Serve immediately. **Yield:** 4 servings.

SHORTCUTS—

- Prepare rice in your microwave first to allow standing time for it to become fluffy and tender.
- Use boneless, tender beef to save preparation time.
- Toast sesame and sunflower seeds in advance, then store, covered, in refrigerator for use as salad toppings.

7

ALL-AMERICAN PIES—they're our favorite dessert...and anytime treat. In a fast-food world, pies say "made with love and patience". No wonder we treat pies (and pie-makers) with such respect!

Inside every pie—in each circle of delicate dough, spoonful of filling, dab of butter, touch of cream or sprinkle of sugar—is the unmistakable mark of a skilled cook.

Our grandmothers were known by their pie-making skills (or lack of them). The reputation of many a modern cook has also been based on her baking skills.

"You should *see* her pies," admirers whisper in reverential tones of blue ribbon bakers. "Her crusts are so light, you'd think they would float away!"

Portable, sweet and satisfying, pies have always been the "stuff" of festive family dinners and the crowd-pleasers at potluck suppers.

But it doesn't take a crowd to appreciate a pie...the most loving words anyone with an appetite can hear may be: "I baked your favorite pie—want a slice?"

COUNTRY PIES. From lower left, clockwise, Banana Cream Chiffon Pie (Pg. 13); Buttermilk Pie (Pg. 14); Rhubarb-Orange Cream Pie (Pg. 14); Pear Crumb Pie (Pg. 15); Pineapple Sour Cream Pie (Pg. 14); French Apple and Walnut Tarts (Pg. 15); Peanut Butter Crunch Pie (Pg. 14); My Mom's Chocolate Pie (Pg. 13).

DESTINED to take their place as family favorites beside traditional pies, these outstanding examples of the pie-maker's art explore new frontiers of flavor.

The Sour Cream Lemon Pie combines farm-fresh dairy products with the tang of lemon... Chocolate Almond Silk Pie is a rich, grown-up treat with its luscious chocolate filling and slivered almonds...Apple Raisin Cream Pie adds a new and creamy twist to an old standby...and Cream Cheese/Pineapple Pie offers an unusual combination of satisfying creaminess contrasting with a sweet and tart pineapple layer.

So, roll out the crust and mix up the filling—you're on your way to baking up a new family favorite!

PICTURE PERFECT PIES. Clockwise from foreground: Sour Cream Lemon Pie (Pg. 15); Chocolate Almond Silk Pie (Pg. 16); Apple Raisin Cream Pie (Pg. 16); and Cream Cheese/Pineapple Pie (Pg. 15).

WINTERY DAY BEAN SOUP
Frances Kissel, New Palestine, Indiana

(PICTURED ON PAGE 4)

- 2 cups mixed dried beans*
- 2 tablespoons salt
- 2 quarts water
- 2 cups diced ham OR sliced smoked sausage
- 1 large onion, chopped
- 1 clove garlic, minced
- 1 teaspoon chili powder
- 1 28-ounce can tomatoes, chopped
- 1 to 2 tablespoons lemon juice

(*Use at least seven varieties of beans —great northern, navy, black, garbanzo, green split peas, pinto and red beans.) Rinse beans; place in large kettle. Cover with water, add salt and soak overnight. Drain; add 2 qts. water and ham/sausage. Simmer for 2-1/2 to 3 hours. Add onion, garlic, chili powder, tomatoes and lemon juice. Simmer 45 minutes. Add salt and pepper, if desired. **Yield:** 2 qts.

CREAM OF BROCCOLI AND CHEESE SOUP
Helen Guida, Tyler, Minnesota

(PICTURED ON PAGE 4)

- 2 cups chopped celery
- 1 cup finely chopped onion
- 1 package (10-ounce) chopped broccoli
- 1 cup cottage cheese
- 2 cups whole milk
- 1 can (10-3/4 ounces) cream of chicken soup, undiluted
- 1/2 teaspoon salt, if desired
- 1/8 teaspoon white pepper

Cook celery, onion and broccoli in 2-1/2 qt. covered casserole in microwave on HIGH for 6 minutes, stirring after 3 minutes. Set aside. Blend cottage cheese in blender or food processor until very smooth; slowly add milk while continuing to blend. Add chicken soup to cheese/milk mixture; blend; add mixture to cooked, undrained vegetables. Microwave on HIGH until heated through (about 3 minutes) *without boiling*. Add salt, pepper. **Yield:** 6 servings.

UPSTATE MINESTRONE SOUP
Yvonne Krantz, Mt. Upton, New York

(PICTURED ON PAGE 4)

- 1 pound Italian sweet sausage
- 1 tablespoon olive OR vegetable oil
- 1 cup diced onion
- 1 clove garlic, finely minced
- 1 cup sliced carrots
- 1 teaspoon crumbled basil
- 2 small zucchini, sliced
- 1 can (1-pound) Italian pear tomatoes, chopped, undrained
- 2 cans (10-3/4-ounce) beef bouillon OR 3 beef bouillon cubes plus 1-1/2 cups hot water
- 2 cups finely shredded cabbage
- 1 teaspoon salt
- 1/4 teaspoon pepper
- 1 can (1-pound) great northern beans, undrained

Chopped fresh parsley

Slice sausage crosswise about 1/2 in. thick; brown in oil in deep saucepan or Dutch oven. Add onion, garlic, carrots and basil; cook for 5 minutes. Add zucchini, tomatoes with liquid, bouillon, cabbage, salt and pepper. Bring soup to boil; reduce heat and simmer, covered, for 1 hour. Add beans with liquid; cook another 20 minutes. Garnish with parsley. (Soup is even better second day!) **Yield:** 8 servings.

FISH AND CHEESE CHOWDER
Pat Paulovich, Manning, Alberta

(PICTURED ON PAGE 4)

- 1 pound fish fillets, fresh or frozen
- 2 tablespoons butter
- 6 tablespoons chopped onion
- 1 cup chopped carrot
- 6 tablespoons chopped celery
- 1/4 cup flour
- 1/2 teaspoon salt, optional

Dash paprika

- 2 10-ounce cans chicken broth, undiluted
- 3 cups milk
- 1 cup grated processed cheese

Thaw frozen fish fillets enough to allow cutting, about 30 minutes. Cut fish in 1-in. cubes. Melt butter in large saucepan; add onion, carrot and celery. Cook until onion is transparent. Blend in flour, salt and paprika. Cook 1 minute, stirring constantly. Gradually add chicken broth and milk. Cook, stirring constantly, until thickened. Add fish; simmer until fish flakes easily (5 minutes for fresh; 10 for frozen). Add cheese; stir until melted. Serve hot. **Yield:** 2-1/2 qts.

GRANDMA'S CHICKEN AND DUMPLING SOUP
Peggy Bremer, Fairmont, Minnesota

(PICTURED ON PAGE 5)

CHICKEN BROTH:
- 1 fryer (2-1/2- to 3-pound) chicken, cut up
- 6 cups cold water
- 3 chicken bouillon cubes
- 6 peppercorns
- 3 whole cloves

SOUP BASE:
- 1 can (10-3/4-ounce) chicken broth
- 1 can (10-3/4-ounce) cream chicken soup
- 1 can (10-3/4-ounce) cream mushroom soup
- 1 cup chopped celery
- 1-1/2 cups chopped carrots
- 1/4 cup chopped onion
- 1 cup chopped potatoes
- 1 small bay leaf
- 1 cup fresh OR frozen peas

Cooked fryer, cut in bite-size pieces
Reserved chicken broth, strained
- 1 teaspoon seasoned salt

FEATHER DUMPLINGS:
- 2 cups flour
- 1 teaspoon salt
- 4 teaspoons baking powder
- 1/4 teaspoon white OR black pepper
- 1 egg, well beaten
- 2 tablespoons melted butter
- 2/3 cup milk

Place fryer, water, bouillon, peppercorns and cloves in kettle and bring to boil. Reduce heat; simmer until chicken is tender (about 1-1/2 hours). Cool chicken just slightly; cut into bite-size pieces and set aside. Strain and skim chicken broth. Put the reserved chicken and broth in large kettle; add cans of broth, chicken and mushroom soups, celery, carrots, onion, potatoes, bay leaf, peas and seasoned salt. Put cover on kettle; simmer soup on low heat for 2-3 hours. About 30 minutes before serving, mix up feather dumplings by sifting dry ingredients together. Add egg, melted butter and enough milk to make moist, stiff batter. Drop by teaspoons into boiling liquid. Cook, covered and without "peeking", for 18-20 minutes or until the dumplings are done. **Yield:** 10-12 servings.

11

CHEDDAR CHOWDER
Laura Rothlisberger, Green, Kansas

(PICTURED ON PAGE 5)

```
2    cups water
2    cups diced potatoes
1/2  cup diced carrots
1/2  cup diced celery
1/4  cup chopped onion
1    teaspoon salt
1/4  teaspoon pepper
```

WHITE SAUCE:
```
1/4  cup butter
1/4  cup flour
2    cups milk
2    cups cheddar cheese, grated
1    cup cubed ham
```

Combine water, potatoes, carrots, celery, onion, salt and pepper in large kettle. Boil 10-12 minutes. Meanwhile, in small saucepan, make white sauce by melting the butter. Add flour and stir until smooth (about 1 minute). Slowly add milk; cook until thickened. Add grated cheese to white sauce; stir until melted. Add white sauce and cubed ham to vegetables that *have not been drained*. Heat through. **Yield:** 6 servings.

CZECHOSLOVAKIAN CABBAGE SOUP
Patricia Rutherford, Winchester, Illinois

(PICTURED ON PAGE 5)

```
2    pounds beef soup bones
1    cup chopped onion
3    carrots, pared and
     coarsely chopped
2    cloves garlic, chopped
1    bay leaf
2    pounds beef short ribs
1    teaspoon dried leaf thyme
1/2  teaspoon paprika
8    cups water
8    cups coarsely chopped
     cabbage (1 head)
2    cans (1-pound) tomatoes
2    teaspoons salt
1/2  to 3/4 teaspoon Tabasco sauce
1/4  cup chopped parsley
3    tablespoons lemon juice
3    tablespoons sugar
1    can (1-pound) sauerkraut
```

Place beef bones, onion, carrots, garlic and bay leaf in roasting pan. Top with short ribs; sprinkle with thyme and paprika. Roast, uncovered, in 450° oven for 20-30 minutes or until meat is brown. Transfer meat and vegetables into large kettle. Using a small amount of water, scrape browned meat bits from roasting pan into kettle. Add water, cabbage, tomatoes, salt and Tabasco. Bring to boil. Cover; simmer 1-1/2 hours. Skim off fat. Add parsley, lemon juice, sugar and sauerkraut. Cook, uncovered, for 1 hour. Remove bones and short ribs from kettle. Cool slightly; remove meat from bones. Cut meat into cubes; return to kettle. Cook 5 minutes longer. **Yield:** 12 servings.

CHEESE AND POTATO WILD RICE SOUP
Gladys Barron, Thief River Falls, Minnesota

(PICTURED ON PAGE 5)

```
1/2    cup wild rice, uncooked
1-1/2  cups water
1/2    pound bacon, cut in pieces
1/4    cup chopped onion
2      10-3/4-ounce cans cream of
       potato soup (dilute with 1
       can liquid—1/2 milk; 1/2
       water)
1      quart milk
2-1/2  cups grated American cheese
```
Carrot curls (optional)

Combine wild rice and water in saucepan and cook over low heat for 45 minutes. Drain. Set aside. Fry bacon pieces and onion in skillet until bacon is crisp. Drain bacon and onion on paper towel. Place soup in large saucepan; dilute as directed above. Stir in milk (1 qt.), bacon, onion, cheese and cooked rice. Stir until cheese is melted. Garnish with carrot. **Yield:** 8-10 servings.

CHICKEN WILD RICE SOUP
Amy Kraemer, Glencoe, Minnesota

```
1      3-pound chicken, cut up and
       rinsed
3      quarts water
1      teaspoon salt
```
Celery leaves (handful)
```
1/2    cup chopped onion
1      carrot, chopped
2      tablespoons butter
3      cups sliced celery
1-1/2  cups chopped onion
2      cups wild rice, rinsed
1/4    teaspoon pepper
1      to 2 teaspoons salt
2      10-3/4-ounce cans cream of
       mushroom soup, undiluted
1/4    teaspoon nutmeg
1/4    teaspoon garlic powder
1      teaspoon instant chicken
       bouillon
```

Arrange cut-up chicken in 6-quart soup kettle. Add water, salt, celery leaves, 1/2 cup onion and carrot. Cook over low heat for 1-1/2 hours or until meat is tender. Strain stock, reserving broth and chicken. Cool chicken; chop into 3/4-in. chunks. Melt butter in skillet; add sliced celery and 1-1/2 cups onion and saute 3 minutes. Place reserved chicken broth (12 cups) back in kettle; add sauteed vegetables, wild rice, pepper and salt. Cook over low heat until rice is tender/crunchy, about 45 minutes. When rice is done, add chopped chicken, mushroom soup, nutmeg, garlic powder and chicken bouillon. Mix gently and heat through, being careful not to scorch (soup is thick). If too thick, add more broth. **Yield:** 5 quarts.

SOUP'S ON
● For rich-seasoned chicken stock, freeze wing tips, necks, any skin or juice/broth. Add to these 1 large chopped onion, 1-2 cups celery leaves, 2 chicken bouillon cubes, 1 chopped carrot and 1 teaspoon salt. Simmer 1 hour; strain and use for broth.

● To prevent curdling in cream soups, use low temperatures and have all ingredients at room temperature.

MAPLE BRAN MUFFINS
Donna Klein-Gebbinck, Elmvale, Ontario

(PICTURED ON PAGE 6)

```
3/4    cup natural wheat bran
1/2    cup milk
1/2    cup maple syrup
1      egg, slightly beaten
1/4    cup oil
1-1/4  cups whole wheat flour
3      teaspoons baking powder
1/2    teaspoon salt
1/3    cup chopped walnuts
```

GLAZE:
```
1      tablespoon butter
1/2    cup confectioners' sugar
1      tablespoon maple syrup
```

Combine bran, milk and maple syrup. Mix in egg and oil. Combine remaining muffin ingredients. Add bran mixture, stirring until just moistened. Divide batter into 12 greased muffin tins. Bake at 400° for 18 to 20 minutes. **Glaze:** Combine ingredients, stirring to blend, and spread over warm muffins.

OATMEAL APPLE RAISIN MUFFINS
Priscilla Weaver, Hagerstown, Maryland

(PICTURED ON PAGE 6)

- 1 egg
- 3/4 cup milk
- 1 cup raisins
- 1 chopped apple
- 1/2 cup oil
- 1 cup all-purpose flour
- 1 cup quick oats
- 1/3 cup sugar
- 3 teaspoons baking powder
- 1 teaspoon salt
- 1 teaspoon nutmeg
- 2 teaspoons cinnamon

Beat egg; stir in remaining ingredients, mixing just to moisten. Pour into 12 greased muffin cups until 3/4 full. Bake at 400° for 15 to 20 minutes. Serve cool or piping hot with butter.

CARROT BRAN MUFFINS
Lorna Jacobsen, Arrowwood, Alberta

(PICTURED ON PAGE 6)

- 3 cups all-purpose flour
- 1 teaspoon baking soda
- 1-1/2 tablespoons baking powder
- 1/2 teaspoon salt, optional
- 1 tablespoon cinnamon
- 2 cups bran
- 4 eggs
- 1-1/2 cups vegetable oil
- 1-1/4 cups dark brown sugar
- 1/4 cup molasses
- 3 cups finely grated carrots
- 1 cup raisins OR currants

Sift together flour, soda, baking powder, salt and cinnamon. Add bran; set aside. Beat eggs; add oil, sugar and molasses. Add carrots, flour mixture and raisins. Fill 24 greased muffin tins 3/4 full. Bake at 350° for 25 minutes. **Yield:** 24 large muffins. **Diabetic Exchanges:** One muffin equals 1 bread, 1 vegetable, 3 fat; also 264 calories, 239 mg sodium with salt (195 mg sodium without salt), 42 mg cholesterol, 31 gm carbohydrates.

POPPY SEED MUFFINS
Germaine Stank, Pound, Wisconsin

(PICTURED ON PAGE 6)

- 3/4 cup sugar
- 1/4 cup softened butter
- 1/2 teaspoon grated orange peel
- 2 eggs
- 2 cups all-purpose flour
- 2-1/2 teaspoons baking powder
- 1/2 teaspoon salt
- 1/4 teaspoon ground nutmeg
- 1 cup milk
- 1/2 cup golden raisins
- 1/2 cup chopped pecans
- 5 tablespoons poppy seeds

Cream sugar, butter and orange peel. Add eggs, one at a time, beating well after each. Combine flour, baking powder, salt and nutmeg. Add to creamed mixture alternately with milk, beating well after each addition. Fold in raisins, nuts and poppy seeds. Spoon batter into greased muffin tins until about 3/4 full. Bake at 400° about 20 minutes. **Yield:** about 16 large muffins.

BANANA CREAM CHIFFON PIE
Anne Wrolstad, Molalla, Oregon

(PICTURED ON PAGE 8)

GRAHAM CRACKER CRUST:
- 1-1/2 cups graham cracker crumbs
- 1/3 cup butter, melted
- 3 tablespoons sugar

FILLING:
- 1 cup top milk (use whole milk with 3 tablespoons cream)
- 3 egg yolks
- 1/4 cup sugar
- 1/4 teaspoon salt
- 1 tablespoon unflavored gelatin
- 1/4 cup cold water
- 1-1/2 teaspoons vanilla
- 3 egg whites
- 1/4 cup sugar
- 3 bananas

TOPPING:
- 1/2 cup whipping cream, whipped

For crust, combine crumbs, butter and sugar in bowl; blend well with fork. Spoon crumb mixture into 9-in. pie pan; set 8-in. pie pan on top and press to make even crumb layer. Remove 8-in. pan. Bake crust at 375° for 8 minutes if desired, or use as is. To make filling, scald milk in top of double boiler. In small bowl, beat egg yolks, sugar and salt. Stir into hot milk; continue cooking until mixture coats spoon (soft custard). Meanwhile, soak gelatin in cold water; let stand 5 minutes. Add to custard along with vanilla; cool mixture over ice water until it thickens. Beat egg whites until foamy; add sugar gradually, beating until stiff. Fold into cooled custard. Set aside. Slice 1 banana over bottom crust. Pour custard over banana slices. Slice 1 banana on top of custard. Beat whipping cream and pile on top of pie. Slice last banana in circles around top. Refrigerate.

MY MOM'S CHOCOLATE PIE
Suzanne Light, Cassville, New York

(PICTURED ON PAGE 8)

- 1 9-inch baked pie shell

CHOCOLATE FILLING:
- 2 to 3 squares (2-3 ounces) unsweetened chocolate
- 2/3 to 1 cup sugar blended with
- 1/2 cup flour
- 2-2/3 cups milk
- 1/4 teaspoon salt
- 1 tablespoon butter
- 4 egg yolks, beaten
- 1 teaspoon vanilla

WHIPPED CREAM TOPPING:
- 1 cup whipping cream, chilled
- 1/4 cup confectioners' sugar
- 1 teaspoon vanilla
- Chocolate curls or leaves to garnish

Melt chocolate in top of double boiler. Add sugar blended with flour, milk, salt and butter to melted chocolate; stir with whisk over hot water until thick. Cook, uncovered, 10 minutes longer. Add 1 cup of chocolate mixture to beaten egg yolks, beating both together. Add chocolate/egg yolk mixture to rest of chocolate filling; cook 5 minutes longer. Remove from heat; add vanilla, stirring to blend. Cool slightly; pour into baked shell. Refrigerate. Make whipped cream topping by placing all ingredients in mixing bowl and beating together until stiff. Pipe onto pie or frost. Top with chocolate curls or leaves, if desired. Store in refrigerator.

RHUBARB-ORANGE CREAM PIE
Wanda Rosseland, Circle, Montana

(PICTURED ON PAGE 8)
1 9-inch *baked* pie shell

FILLING:
1-1/2 cups sugar
2 tablespoons cornstarch
3 cups fresh rhubarb, cut in 1/2-inch pieces (can use frozen)
1/2 cup cream, half and half OR milk
1/4 cup orange juice
5 drops red food coloring (optional)
3 egg yolks, slightly beaten

MERINGUE:
3 egg whites
1/4 teaspoon cream of tartar
3 tablespoons sugar
1/2 teaspoon vanilla

Combine sugar, cornstarch, rhubarb, cream/milk, orange juice and food coloring in medium saucepan. Cook over medium heat stirring frequently until rhubarb is tender and mixture has thickened. Pour 1 cup hot rhubarb mixture into egg yolks, stirring constantly. Add to rest of hot rhubarb mixture; bring to boil. Cool slightly; pour filling into pie shell. Make meringue by beating egg whites and cream of tartar until soft peaks form. Slowly add sugar and vanilla, beating until stiff peaks form. Spread over filling, sealing edges. Bake at 350° for 12 minutes or until golden brown.

BUTTERMILK PIE
Carol Bown, Currie, Minnesota

(PICTURED ON PAGE 8)
4 eggs
1-1/2 to 2 cups sugar
6 tablespoons butter, melted
2 tablespoons flour
1 teaspoon vanilla
1/2 teaspoon salt
3/4 cup buttermilk
1 9-inch *unbaked* pie shell
1/3 cup walnuts, chopped

Beat eggs in medium bowl with electric mixer. Add sugar, butter, flour, vanilla and salt. Reduce mixer speed; slowly add buttermilk and blend well. Pour filling into pie shell. Sprinkle walnuts on top. Bake at 350° for 40-45 minutes or until knife comes out clean and top is golden. Keep refrigerated.

PINEAPPLE SOUR CREAM PIE
Ella Gipman, Choiceland, Saskatchewan

(PICTURED ON PAGE 9)
1 9-inch graham cracker crust*

FILLING:
1/3 to 1/2 cup sugar
1/4 cup flour
1/2 teaspoon salt
2-1/2 cups crushed pineapple, undrained
1 cup cultured sour cream
1 tablespoon lemon juice
2 egg yolks, slightly beaten

MERINGUE:
2 egg whites
1/4 teaspoon cream of tartar
1/4 cup sugar

*Use crust recipe from Banana Cream Chiffon Pie recipe. Combine sugar, flour and salt in medium saucepan. Stir in pineapple, sour cream and lemon juice; cook over medium heat, stirring, until mixture comes to boil. Cook 2 minutes. Stir 1/2 cup of cooked mixture into beaten egg yolks; return filling/egg yolk mixture to remaining filling. Cook for 2 minutes more, stirring constantly. Cool slightly. Spoon filling into crust. Make meringue by beating egg whites with cream of tartar until soft peaks form. Add sugar gradually, beating until stiff peaks form. Spread over pie filling; seal edges. Bake at 350° for 12-15 minutes or until golden brown.

PEANUT BUTTER CRUNCH PIE
Joey Ann Mostowy, Bruin, Pennsylvania

(PICTURED ON PAGE 9)
1 10-inch *baked* pie shell
1/2 cup crunchy peanut butter
2/3 cup confectioners' sugar

CREAM FILLING:
2/3 cup sugar
3 tablespoons cornstarch
1 tablespoon flour
1/2 teaspoon salt
3 egg yolks
3 cups milk
2 tablespoons butter
1 teaspoon vanilla

MERINGUE:
3 egg whites
1/4 cup sugar
1/4 teaspoon cream of tartar
1 teaspoon cornstarch

Combine peanut butter and sugar until crumbly; spread over bottom of pie shell *reserving 2 tablespoons for decoration*. Make filling by combining sugar, cornstarch, flour, salt, egg yolks, milk and butter in medium saucepan; bring to boil, stirring constantly. Cook for 2 minutes. Remove from heat; add vanilla. Pour cream filling over peanut crunch layer. Make meringue by beating egg whites until foamy; add remaining ingredients gradually, beating until whites are smooth and stiff. Spread over cream filling, sealing edges. Top with remaining peanut/sugar mixture. Bake at 350° for about 10 minutes or until meringue is lightly browned.

PIE TIPS
● Store flour in the freezer and use chilled flour in pie dough. This eliminates chilling dough and gives tender, flaky crusts.
● To prevent overbrowning and oven spillovers, make a *pie skirt* by cutting a 2-in. strip of foil 2 in. longer than the circumference of pie tin. Wrap around pie; lap edges. Push foil against pie pan sides below the edge; let top edge stand up.
● To eliminate soggy crusts on custard pies, roll one opened, unbeaten egg around pie crust to seal it. Use egg later in custard filling.
● For a golden brown crust, brush pie top (not edges) with cream or milk before

baking. Sprinkle with sugar if desired.

● For flaky pastry, handle dough as *little* as possible. Overhandling toughens dough.

● Roll pastry from center out to edges —never roll back over dough toward center. This keeps dough even in size and thickness.

● When making meringues, have eggs at room temperature for best volume. Use grease-free utensils and *do not use plastic bowls.* Egg whites must have no trace of yolk. Don't use super-fresh eggs straight from the hen-house—older eggs whip better.

● Prevent shrinking meringues by carefully sealing to pastry edges on top of hot pie filling.

● Cool meringue pies to room temperature before refrigerating. Cooling too quickly may cause shrinkage or sticky, beaded meringues.

● To cut meringue without tearing, dip your knife in cold water first.

PEAR CRUMB PIE
Edna Hoffman, Hebron, Indiana

(PICTURED ON PAGE 9)

1 9-inch, *unbaked* pie shell with high fluted edge, chilled

PEAR FILLING:
2-1/2 pounds fresh, ripe pears (Bosc, Anjou or Bartlett)
1 tablespoon lemon juice
2/3 cup sugar
1 teaspoon cinnamon
1/4 teaspoon mace
1 to 2 tablespoons flour

TOPPING:
1 cup flour
1/3 cup light brown sugar
1/3 cup butter, softened

Peel, core and slice pears in large bowl; sprinkle with lemon juice. Combine sugar, spices and flour in small bowl; sprinkle over pears and toss lightly to mix. Spoon filling into prepared pie shell. Combine topping ingredients; sprinkle over filling. Bake at 375° for 40-45 minutes or until juice bubbles up and top lightly browns. (Cover top loosely with piece of foil if it browns too quickly.) Cool.

FRENCH APPLE AND WALNUT TARTS
Rosemary Neeb, Crediton, Ontario

(PICTURED ON PAGE 9)

TARTS:
1/2 cup soft butter
1/2 cup sugar
2 large eggs
3/4 cup flour blended with
1/2 teaspoon baking powder
2 tablespoons milk
1/2 cup walnuts, coarsely chopped

FILLING:
4 to 5 apples
2 to 3 tablespoons butter, melted
Confectioners' sugar

In medium mixing bowl, beat butter until light and fluffy; gradually beat in sugar. Add eggs, one at a time, beating until smooth. Fold in flour blended with baking powder. Stir in milk and chopped walnuts. Set aside. Butter 6-8 individual tart tins or Texas-size muffin tins; divide batter mixture evenly between them. Peel, quarter and core apples. Cut each quarter into thin, even slices. Stand apple slices in batter (rounded side up), pressing down lightly so they are all level. Brush with butter. Bake (on cookie sheet, if individual tarts) at 375° for 25 minutes or until golden brown. Cool for 3-5 minutes. *Gently* lift from pans. Just before serving, dust with confectioners' sugar. **Yield:** 6-8 tarts.

'BERRY' NICE GLAZE
● To get a clear, seedless strawberry glaze for fresh strawberry pie, mash and strain the berries to get juice for glaze. (You'll need to add berries to compensate for lost pulp.)

CREAM CHEESE-PINEAPPLE PIE
Elizabeth Brown, Clayton, Delaware

(PICTURED ON PAGE 10)

PINEAPPLE LAYER:
1/3 cup sugar
1 tablespoon cornstarch
1 can (8 ounces) crushed pineapple with juice

CREAM CHEESE LAYER:
1 package (8 ounces) cream cheese, softened to room temperature
1/2 cup sugar
1 teaspoon salt
2 eggs
1/2 cup milk
1/2 teaspoon vanilla
1 9-inch *unbaked* pie shell
1/4 cup chopped pecans

Combine sugar, cornstarch and pineapple plus juice in a small saucepan. Cook over medium heat, stirring constantly until mixture is thick and clear. Cool; set aside. Blend cream cheese, sugar and salt in mixer bowl. Add 2 eggs, one at a time, beating after each addition. Blend in milk and vanilla. (If mixture looks slightly curdled, don't worry—it bakes out.) Spread cooled pineapple layer over bottom of pie shell. Pour cream cheese mixture over pineapple; sprinkle with pecans. Bake at 400° for 10 minutes; reduce heat to 325° and bake for 50 minutes. Cool.

SOUR CREAM LEMON PIE
Martha Sorenson, Fallon, Nevada

(PICTURED ON PAGE 10)

1 cup sugar
3-1/2 tablespoons cornstarch
1 tablespoon lemon rind, grated
1/2 cup fresh lemon juice
3 egg yolks, slightly beaten
1 cup milk
1/4 cup butter
1 cup cultured sour cream
1 *baked* 9-inch pie shell
1 cup heavy whipping cream, whipped
Lemon twists for garnish

Combine sugar, cornstarch, lemon rind, juice, egg yolks and milk in heavy saucepan; cook over medium heat until thick. Stir in butter and cool mixture to room temperature. Stir in sour cream and pour filling into pie shell. Cover with whipped cream and garnish with lemon twists. Store in refrigerator.

CHOCOLATE ALMOND SILK PIE
Diane Larson, Rolad, Iowa

(PICTURED ON PAGE 10)

CRUST:
- 1 cup flour
- 1/4 cup finely chopped toasted almonds
- 6 tablespoons butter
- 3 tablespoons confectioners' sugar
- 1/4 teaspoon vanilla

FILLING:
- 1 cup sugar
- 3/4 cup softened butter
- 3 squares (1 ounce each) unsweetened chocolate, melted and cooled
- 1/4 to 1/2 teaspoon almond extract OR 2-3 tablespoons almond-flavored liqueur
- 3 eggs

Sweetened whipped cream
Toasted sliced almonds

Combine all crust ingredients and blend with mixer on low speed until well mixed, 2-3 minutes. Press on bottom and sides of 9-in. pie pan; bake at 400° for 8-10 minutes. Cool. To make filling, combine sugar and butter in small mixer bowl; beat at medium speed until light and fluffy. Add chocolate and almond extract/liqueur; beat until well mixed. Add eggs one at a time, beating 2 minutes after each addition. Spoon filling into cooled crust; refrigerate until firm, 3-4 hours. Garnish with whipped cream and sliced almonds. Keep refrigerated.

APPLE RAISIN CREAM PIE
Carolina Hofeldt, Lloyd, Montana

(PICTURED ON PAGE 10)

Pastry for 2-crust, 10-inch pie

FILLING:
- 7 to 8 cups tart apple slices, 1/8 inch thick
- 1 cup sugar
- 1/2 cup flour
- 1/2 teaspoon nutmeg
- 1 teaspoon cinnamon
- 3/4 cup raisins

Dash salt, if desired
- 1 to 2 teaspoons grated lemon rind
- 1 tablespoon (rounded) butter
- 3/4 cup heavy cream

Make favorite pastry; line bottom of pie tin with one crust and set aside. Combine apple slices, sugar, flour, spices, raisins, salt and lemon peel; mix together well. Spoon filling into pastry-lined pan; dot with butter. Cover with top crust decorated with steam vents; seal edges. Cut a 1-in. circle from dough in center of top crust. Bake at 400° for 40-45 minutes. Remove pie from oven; slowly pour cream into center hole of top crust. Return to oven; bake 5-10 minutes longer. Let stand 5 minutes before cutting. (Refrigerate leftovers.)

GRANDMA'S SOUR CREAM RAISIN PIE
Beverly Medalen, Willow City, North Dakota

- 1 9-inch baked pie shell
- 1 cup raisins (water enough to cover)
- 2/3 cup sugar
- 3 tablespoons cornstarch
- 1/8 teaspoon salt
- 1/8 teaspoon ground cloves
- 1/2 teaspoon ground cinnamon
- 1 cup sour cream
- 3 egg yolks
- 1/2 cup milk
- 1/2 cup water (drained off plumped raisins)
- 1/2 cup nuts, chopped (optional)

MERINGUE:
- 3 egg whites
- 1/4 teaspoon salt
- 5 tablespoons sugar

Place raisins in small saucepan. Add water to cover; bring to boil. Turn off heat. Let stand while preparing filling. In heavy saucepan, mix together sugar, cornstarch, salt, cloves and cinnamon. Add sour cream; stir well. Beat in egg yolks. Stir in milk and cook on medium heat, stirring until pudding comes to boil and is pudding consistency (mixture will be thick). Remove from heat. Drain raisins, reserving 1/2 cup liquid. Stir liquid into filling; add raisins, nuts and pour into pie shell. Prepare meringue by beating egg whites with salt until foamy. Gradually add sugar while continuing to beat on high. Beat until stiff and glossy. Spread over pie, making sure meringue covers all of pie filling. Bake at 350° for 10-15 minutes or until light golden brown. Remove from oven. Serve warm or cold. **Yield:** 8 servings.

GOLDEN COCONUT PEACH PIE

- 4 to 4-1/2 cups sliced, fresh peaches
- 1/2 cup sugar
- 3 tablespoons flour
- 1/4 teaspoon nutmeg
- 1/8 teaspoon salt
- 1/4 cup orange juice
- 1 9-inch unbaked pie shell
- 2 tablespoons butter
- 2 cups flaked coconut
- 1/2 cup evaporated milk
- 1 egg, beaten
- 1/4 to 1/2 cup sugar
- 1/4 teaspoon almond extract

Mix together peaches, sugar, flour, nutmeg, salt and orange juice in medium bowl. Pour mixture into pie shell. Dot with butter; bake at 450° for 15 minutes. Meanwhile, combine coconut, milk, egg, sugar and almond. Pour over hot peach mixture. Reduce heat to 350° and bake until coconut is toasted, about 30 minutes. Chill pie unless eaten at once.

CHRISTMAS MORNING CRANBERRY MUFFINS
Keren Fuller, St. Mary's, Ontario

- 1 cup fresh cranberries
- 1/4 cup sugar
- 1-1/2 cups all-purpose flour
- 1/4 cup sugar
- 2 teaspoons baking powder
- 1 teaspoon salt
- 1/2 teaspoon cinnamon
- 1/4 teaspoon ground allspice
- 1 egg, beaten
- 1/4 teaspoon grated orange peel
- 3/4 cup orange juice
- 1/3 cup butter, melted
- 1/4 cup chopped walnuts

Coarsely chop cranberries. Sprinkle with 1/4 cup sugar and set aside. In bowl, stir together flour, sugar, baking powder, salt, cinnamon and allspice. Make a well in center of dry ingredients. Combine egg, peel, juice and butter. Add all at once to flour mixture; stir to moisten. Fold in cranberry mixture and nuts. Fill greased muffin cups; bake at 375° for 15-20 minutes or until golden. **Yield:** 12 large muffins.

OAT BRAN MUFFINS
Margaret Stricker, Charleston, Missouri

MUFFINS:
- 1 cup oat bran cereal, uncooked
- 1 cup unbleached flour
- 1/3 cup brown sugar, firmly packed
- 1-1/2 teaspoons baking powder
- 1 teaspoon baking soda
- 1/2 teaspoon salt
- 1/2 teaspoon cinnamon
- 3/4 cup orange juice (can include pulp)
- 1/3 cup vegetable oil
- 1 egg
- 1 teaspoon grated orange peel

TOPPING:
- 5 teaspoons oat bran cereal or flour
- 1/4 cup firmly packed brown sugar
- 1/4 cup nuts, finely chopped
- 1/4 teaspoon cinnamon
- 2 tablespoons melted butter or oil

Combine cereal, flour, sugar, baking powder, soda, salt and cinnamon. Add juice (and pulp), oil, egg and orange peel, stirring just until moistened. Fill 12 lightly oiled or paper-lined muffin tins 3/4 full. Bake at 400° for 20 minutes or until golden brown. **Yield: 12 muffins.**

SKIERS FRENCH TOAST
Linda Furney, Shelby, Ohio

- 2 tablespoons corn syrup
- 1/2 cup butter
- 1 cup brown sugar
- 1 loaf unsliced, firm white bread* (trim crusts)
- 5 eggs
- 1-1/2 cups milk
- 1 teaspoon vanilla
- 1/4 teaspoon salt

(*Homemade bread or bread of similar texture is ideal.) Combine syrup, butter and sugar in saucepan; simmer until syrup-like. Pour mixture over bottom of 9- x 13-in. pan. Slice bread into 12-16 slices; place over syrup, layering as needed. Beat together eggs, milk, vanilla and salt. Pour over bread; cover. Refrigerate overnight. Bake, uncovered, at 350° for 45 minutes. Cut in squares, invert and serve with applesauce and breakfast sausage. **Yield: 8 servings.**

APPLE PUFF PANCAKE
Gloria Shelton, Oakes, North Dakota

- 4 tablespoons butter
- 2 large apples, peeled, cored, sliced thin
- 3 tablespoons brown sugar
- 1 teaspoon cinnamon

PANCAKE:
- 6 eggs, room temperature
- 1-1/2 cups milk
- 1 cup flour
- 3 tablespoons sugar
- 1 teaspoon vanilla
- 1/2 teaspoon salt
- 1/2 teaspoon cinnamon

Melt butter in 9- x 13-in. baking pan in 375° oven. Arrange apples over butter; return to oven until apples are soft (about 10 minutes). Sprinkle apples with brown sugar, cinnamon. Combine pancake ingredients in blender; pour over apples. Bake for 30-40 minutes. Sprinkle with powdered sugar. **Yield:** 8 servings. **Diabetic Exchanges:** One serving equals 1 protein, 1-1/2 breads, 1/2 fruit, 1 fat; also 274 mg sodium, 213 mg cholesterol, 248 calories, 27 gm carbohydrate.

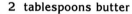

MEXICAN EGGS
Laura Rothlisberger, Green, Kansas

- 2 tablespoons butter
- 1/2 cup chopped onion
- 1/2 cup chopped green pepper
- 8 eggs
- 1/4 cup milk
- 1 teaspoon seasoned salt
- 1/2 teaspoon crushed basil
- 1/4 teaspoon pepper
- 1 package (3-ounce) cream cheese, cubed
- 1 medium tomato, chopped
- 2 to 4 slices bacon, cooked crisp, crumbled

Melt butter in large skillet over medium heat; add onion and green pepper. Cook until tender; set aside. Beat eggs, milk and seasonings. Pour over onion/pepper mixture. Add cheese and tomato. Return skillet to heat. Gently push pancake turner completely across bottom and sides of skillet, forming large soft curds. Cook until eggs are thickened throughout, but still moist. Sprinkle with bacon. **Yield:** 4 servings.

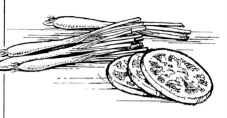

BARBARA'S FARM COFFEE CAKE
Doreen Gerrish, Pawcatuck, Connecticut

- 2 packages active dry yeast
- 1/2 cup water (110°-115°)
- 1-1/2 cups milk, scalded
- 1/2 cup butter
- 1/2 cup honey
- 2 teaspoons salt
- 2 eggs
- 7 to 7-1/2 cups all-purpose flour

WALNUT FILLING:
- 1 cup brown sugar, packed
- 1/2 cup chopped walnuts
- 2 teaspoons ground cinnamon
- 1/2 cup raisins

Dissolve yeast in warm water. In separate large mixing bowl, combine milk, butter, honey and salt. When yeast mixture has cooled to lukewarm, combine it with eggs, 3 cups of flour and milk mixture. Beat until smooth using electric mixer. Stir in enough remaining flour to make soft dough. Knead on floured surface until smooth and elastic, about 10 minutes. Place in greased bowl. Cover; let rise in warm place until doubled, about 1-1/4 hours. Punch down dough. Divide into six pieces. Roll out each to 26- x 4-in. rectangle and sprinkle with 1/6 of filling. Roll up like jelly roll, starting from long edge. Repeat with remaining dough. To form each coffee cake (recipe makes two), coil together (like braided rug) three rolls on greased baking sheet. Cut slits in top of coil every 2 in. with scissors. Let rise until doubled, about 1 hour. Bake at 375° for 20 minutes or until golden. Cool partially on rack; drizzle with a thin confectioners' sugar glaze.

Country Inns

Patchwork Quilt Country Inn
11748 County Road 2, Middlebury, Indiana 46540, 219/825-2417

Directions: Exit Indiana Toll Road at Middlebury (Exit no. 107); north 1/4 mile on Highway 12; west 1 mi. on County Road #2.

Schedule: Open year-round except Sunday, Monday and holidays.

Rates: Amish Back Roads tour with lunch $22.50 per person. Bed and breakfast Tues.-Fri. (3 rooms, shared bath) $49.95 for two. Country Getaway: Five-course din-ner and overnight stay $88.35 for two. Country Sojourn: Lunch, tour, dinner and overnight stay $148.00 per couple sharing room. All rates include continental breakfast. Sales tax not included in rates.

Visa, MasterCard and personal checks accepted.

Policy: No smoking; no alcohol served or permitted on premises. Hours and rates subject to change. Please call or write.

SITUATED on a working farm in the Amish country of northern Indiana, the Patchwork Quilt Country Inn features hearty Amish-style food.

A typical lunch could include tasty ham loaf baked with a tangy tomato sauce glaze, sweet potatoes and home-made applesauce and rolls.

Dinner guests choose the entree in advance for their five-course family-style dinner. Known best for its Butter-milk Pecan Chicken, Burgundy Steak and Baked Ham, the inn's menu also offers poultry and seafood dishes.

Dinner also includes soup, and the Gourmet Buffet, a bountiful board of assorted salads, homemade pickles, relishes, cheese and crackers, bread pudding, tossed salad and more!

Accompanying the entrees are sau-teed cabbage, mashed potatoes with gravy and homemade rolls, jam and apple butter—all fresh and delicious!

The Patchwork Quilt has shared some of its best recipes so you can try them yourself:

AMISH DRESSING

- 18 slices toasted bread, cut in 1/2 inch cubes
- 2 cups diced *cooked* potatoes
- 1 cup shredded carrots
- 3 cups diced celery
- 1/2 cup chopped parsley
- 6 eggs, well beaten
- 1 quart chicken stock
- 2 cups cooked diced chicken

In large bowl, combine bread cubes, potatoes, carrots, celery and parsley. Add beaten eggs and chicken stock. Fold in diced chicken; mix all ingredients until blended. Bake at 350° in well-buttered 13-in. x 9-in. x 2-in. pan for 45-50 minutes until firm. **Yield:** 12-16 servings.

TREVA'S BRIDES PUDDING

- 5 tablespoons unflavored gelatin
- 1 cup cold water
- 3-1/2 cups unbeaten egg whites
- 2 cups sugar
- 3 teaspoons vanilla
- 2 cups shredded coconut
- 4 cups nondairy whipped topping

Garnish—toasted coconut

Soak gelatin in cold water in small saucepan for several minutes until softened. Melt over low heat until gelatin is dissolved. Set aside. Beat egg whites until stiff. Continue beating and slowly add sugar. Beat until soft peaks form. Set aside. Combine gelatin mixture and vanilla. Mix together with egg white mixture. Combine coconut and topping. Gently fold into egg white mixture. Pour into 3 oiled 6-cup molds. Refrigerate until firm. Unmold onto plate; garnish with toasted coconut. **Yield:** 24 servings.

BREAD PUDDING

PUDDING:
- 4 eggs, beaten
- 2 cups brown sugar
- 4-1/2 cups milk
- 3 teaspoons vanilla
- 2 teaspoons cinnamon
- 1 teaspoon salt
- 12 cups bread cubes (use left-over rolls)

SAUCE:
- 3 cups water
- 2 cups raisins
- 3 packages (3 ounces *each*) *instant* vanilla pudding mix
- 3 cups water
- 2 tablespoons lemon juice

Combine eggs, sugar, milk, vanilla, cinnamon and sugar in large bowl. Stir in bread cubes. Pour into buttered 13-in. x 9-in. x 2-in. baking pan. Bake at 350° for 45 minutes. Prepare sauce by simmering water and raisins together until plumped. Reserve water and raisins. In bowl, combine pudding mix with 3 cups water, lemon juice, reserved raisins/water. Stir until mixture thickens. Serve with bread pudding. **Yield:** 16 servings.

BECOMING a good cook is a necessity when you're raising six children, according to Anna Mary Neff of Manheim, Pennsylvania. And one of those six children, Debrah Mossimann of Lititz, Penn., showed her appreciation of her mother's cooking by nominating her as "Best Cook in the Country".

"Anna Mary's splendid food has not only tempted her family and friends, but visitors from all over the world," Debrah wrote. "Through the years, Paul and Anna Mary have entertained people from many countries, especially students who had nowhere to go during the holidays.

"She serves roast beef, flavorful poor man's goose, potato filling, homegrown fresh vegetables, savory oven paprika potatoes, her own chow-chow, cranberry relish, homebaked breads and potato rolls fresh from the oven. Top that off with her special shoo-fly pie and an almond cookie frozen dessert or cracker pudding and you have a meal that remains a wonderful memory for years.

"Why is her food so good? She was a 'natural' cook long before being natural was 'in'. Her food is made from scratch without being complicated. Its uniqueness is all in a spice, an ingredient or technique."

SHOO FLY PIE

CRUMB MIXTURE:
- 2/3 cup brown sugar
- 1 cup flour
- 1 tablespoon shortening

SYRUP MIXTURE:
- 1 cup molasses syrup
- 1 tablespoon unsulphured cooking molasses
- 1 egg, beaten
- 3/4 cup boiling water
- 1 teaspoon baking soda
- 1 9-inch *unbaked* pie shell

Combine crumb mixture, reserving one-half of crumbs for top of pie. Mix syrup, molasses, egg, water and soda together; add crumbs and combine lightly. (Mixture will be lumpy.) Pour into pie shell. Sprinkle reserved crumbs on top. Bake at 375° for 15 minutes with a foil collar around crust. Remove foil. Bake 20 minutes more. Serve with vanilla or butter pecan ice cream.

CHRISTMAS PLUM PUDDING

- 1 egg
- 2/3 cup milk
- 1 cup sugar
- 1 cup flour
- 1 teaspoon baking soda
- 1/2 teaspoon cinnamon
- 1/2 teaspoon nutmeg
- 1 cup ground beef suet, about 4 ounces
- 1 cup raisins
- 1/2 cup chopped nuts, optional
- 1/2 cup currants

VANILLA SAUCE:
- 1 cup water
- 1/2 cup sugar
- 1 tablespoon cornstarch
- 1 teaspoon vanilla
- 1 tablespoon butter
- Pinch salt

Beat egg in mixing bowl, add milk and sugar. Combine flour, baking soda, cinnamon and nutmeg; add to egg mixture, stirring to blend. Cream suet with mixer; add to batter. Stir in raisins, nuts and currants. Mix well. Put in greased 2-qt. mold, cover tightly with foil. Place in deep kettle on rack or canning rings. Add boiling water to 1-inch depth. Cover kettle. Boil gently, replacing water as needed. Steam for 2 hours. Let stand for 10 minutes; unmold to plate. Make sauce by combining sugar and cornstarch; stir in water. Stir in vanilla, butter and salt after removing from heat. Serve warm on pudding. **Yield:** 8-10 servings.

POTATO FILLING

- 6 cups mashed potatoes
- 3 eggs
- 1-1/2 cups milk
- 2 cups dry bread crumbs
- 1/2 cup chopped onions
- 1 cup chopped celery
- 2 tablespoons butter
- 1/4 cup chopped parsley
- Salt
- Pepper
- Saffron, optional, very small amount soaked in 1/4 cup water

Cook potatoes in boiling salted water until tender; drain. Mash. Add eggs, milk and bread crumbs to potatoes. Set aside. Saute onions and celery in butter. Add to potato mixture. Add parsley, salt, pepper and saffron, if desired. Mix well. Put in greased 2-1/2 qt. casserole. Bake at 350°, uncovered, for 1 hour. **Yield:** 12 servings. (Also makes potato patties, lightly sauteed in butter or margarine.) A good use for leftover mashed potatoes.

CRANBERRY RELISH

- 1 12-oz. bag frozen cranberries
- 1 orange
- 6 to 8 red-skinned apples
- 1 can (20 ounces) crushed pineapple
- 1 cup sugar

Grind cranberries, orange and apples together. Add pineapple and sugar, stirring to blend. Store mixture for short time in refrigerator; may also be frozen. **Yield:** 4-5 cups.

PIONEER FARE, These are hearty foods of the type that sustained our ancestors on their westward journey. They became regional favorites—and are now old standbys found on tables across the country. You'll probably recognize some dishes from *your* part of the country.

Our buckboard seat displays these flavorful foods—a variety of corn dishes, rich baked beans, distinctive salads and side dishes, dark bread, wild game and highly seasoned-and-sauced meat. Rediscover these time-honored classics ...for a real "taste of the country"!

FRONTIER FOOD. Clockwise from lower left: Hot Bacon Dressing with Spinach (Pg. 27); Michigan Bean Bake (Pg. 27); Creole Corn Muffins (Pg. 27); Big Sky Country Ribs (Pg. 27); Anadama Bread (Pg. 28); Baked Corn (Pg. 28); North Woods Wild Fowl and Sauce (Pg. 27); and Wild Rice Side Dish (Pg. 27. (Last two dishes shown combined.)

SUNDAY DESSERTS. These are the kind that Grandma used to make for Sundays and special occasions.

Made of common ingredients and seasonal orchard bounty, these pies, cakes, kuchens and cookies were the "stuff" of Grandma's kitchen!

Close your eyes...imagine fresh peeled lemon rind...the nutty goodness of hickory trees...the sweet-tart taste of pie cherries...and the sharp, spiced fragrance of molasses spice cookies.

Relive those memories today with our sampling of regional sweet treats. One taste will take you home again!

PASS THE DESSERT! Clockwise from lower left: Lemon 'N Apple Chess Pie (Pg. 28); Grandma's Hickory Nut Cake (Pg. 28); Molasses Crinkle Cookies (Pg. 29); Fruit Muerbeting (Custard Kuchen) (Pg. 29).

Meals in Minutes

Recipes from Grace Howaniec, Waukesha, Wisconsin.

DELICIOUS...nutritious...and *fast*. That's the beauty of this ready-in-less-than-30-minutes meal. Enjoy the savory flavor of lime/dill marinade on the boneless chicken breast and the palate-pleasing tang of the vinaigrette dressing that highlights the spinach/orange salad. And for dessert, the simple-but-satisfying combination of fresh strawberries and shortbread cookies is sure to be a hit!

By the way, you can save even more time by using a purchased salad dressing, but by making your own, you have the opportunity to control the amount of salt, sugar and oil in the dressing—an added bonus!

GRILLED CHICKEN BREASTS WITH LIME/DILL SAUCE

4 chicken breast *halves*, deboned and skinned

MARINADE:
- 1/4 cup lime juice (may use lemon)
- 1/4 teaspoon salt
- 1/8 teaspoon pepper
- 1/2 teaspoon dried dill weed
- 1/2 teaspoon dried minced onion
- 2 tablespoons melted butter

Combine all marinade ingredients in heavy zip-lock plastic bag; mix. Add chicken breasts; seal bag. Turn to coat chicken with marinade; let stand at room temperature for 10-15 minutes. Meanwhile, pre-heat charcoal grill. Place chicken breasts over medium coals or low setting on gas grill. Cover grill; grill for 5 minutes on each side. (Chicken can also be oven-broiled.) Baste with butter after turning. Serve hot with buttered noodles. **Yield:** 4 servings.

Prepare Poultry Properly!

- Always rinse raw poultry thoroughly inside and out under cold running water.

- When cutting raw poultry, use a plastic or ceramic surface (one that can be washed in the dishwasher or else scrubbed in hot, soapy water and chlorine bleach).
- Wash knives and surfaces that come in contact with raw poultry with a bleach-based detergent. Use disposable paper towels to wipe up poultry juices.

SPINACH/ORANGE SALAD WITH VINAIGRETTE DRESSING

Fresh spinach leaves, washed, drained on paper towels and chilled
2 oranges, peeled and sliced into 1/2-inch slices

VINAIGRETTE DRESSING:
- 3 tablespoons vegetable oil
- 1 tablespoon white vinegar OR white wine
- 1/2 teaspoon sugar
- 1 teaspoon lemon juice
- 1/4 teaspoon dry mustard
- 1/4 teaspoon salt
- 1/8 teaspoon pepper

Place spinach leaves on individual plates (or in one large salad bowl to save time). Garnish with orange slices. Immediately before serving, top with dressing made by combining all ingredients together in covered container and mixing well. **Yield:** 4 servings.

FRESH STRAWBERRY CUP

1 quart fresh strawberries, rinsed, drained and sliced
Confectioners' sugar, if desired
Shortbread cookies

Arrange strawberry slices in dessert bowls; sprinkle with sugar. Mix gently. Serve with cookies. **Yield:** 4 servings.

VERSATILE zucchini is easily the "most compatible" vegetable in any backyard garden—it finds its way into a surprising variety of dishes!

Good eating begins and ends with zucchini, from crisp, oven-baked zucchini strip appetizers... to sliced zucchini rounds in a cheese soup...to grated zucchini, beef and herbs in a delightful summer meat loaf.

And zucchini-laden cakes, cookies and breads satisfy sweet cravings!

ADAPTABLE ZUCCHINI. Clockwise from lower left: Cheese Zucchini Crisps (Pg. 29); Cheese Zucchini Soup (Pg. 29); Quick Zucchini Cake (Pg. 30); Zucchini Lemon Butter (Pg. 31); Zucchini Fudge Cake (Pg. 30); Zucchini/Granola Cookies (Pg. 30); Zucchini Parmesan Bread (Pg. 31); Zucchini Meat Loaf (Pg. 30).

AMAZING, abundant zucchini—you just have to admire a vegetable that tries so hard to please!

What other vegetable can dress up a stir-fry...crunch up a salad ...moisten a fudge cake...or nestle comfortably in a casserole—and do it all so tastefully?

If you're among those who like the fresh, light taste of zucchini in simply prepared dishes, you'll enjoy Zucchini in Dill Cream Sauce.

If you prefer your zucchini "in disguise", try Zucchini Lemon Butter or Zucchini Parmesan Bread. Whichever way, there's a lot to like about zucchini...and *a lot* of zucchini recipes you'll like.

ZESTY ZUCCHINI! Italian Sausage and Zucchini Stir Fry (Pg. 31); Zucchini Casserole (Pg. 31); Zucchini in Dill Cream Sauce (Pg. 32); Italian Zucchini Salad (Pg. 32).

NORTH WOODS WILD FOWL & SAUCE

Mabel Haugen, Tomahawk, Wisconsin

(PICTURED ON PAGE 20)

Pheasant, quail, grouse, guinea hen or other wild fowl

NORTH WOODS SAUCE:
- 1/4 cup finely chopped onion
- 2 tablespoons vegetable oil
- 1 tablespoon cornstarch
- 1 cup chicken broth (or 2 teaspoons chicken bouillon dissolved in 1 cup water)
- 1 teaspoon brown sugar
- 1 teaspoon grated orange peel
- 1/4 cup orange juice
- 1 cup fresh seedless grapes
- 1/4 teaspoon crushed fennel seed
- 2 tablespoons chopped fresh or dried parsley

Roast fowl, covered, in oven at 300° until nearly done OR cut fowl in serving pieces and coat with mixture of 1/2 cup finely crushed cornflakes, 1/4 cup flour, salt and pepper. Fry in 2 tablespoons vegetable oil until tender. Set aside. Make sauce by sauteing onion in oil until transparent. Stir in cornstarch, broth, brown sugar and orange peel. Bring mixture to boil, stirring as it thickens. Add orange juice, grapes, parsley, fennel and salt, if desired. Pour over fried fowl in oven casserole; bake at 350° for 12 minutes. Roasted fowl can be brushed with sauce and returned to oven at 325° to complete cooking. **Yield:** Each pheasant serves 2.

WILD RICE CASSEROLE

Gladys Barron, Thief River Falls, Minnesota

(PICTURED ON PAGE 20)

- 1/4 cup butter
- 1/4 cup chopped onion
- 1 cup uncooked wild rice
- 8 ounces fresh mushrooms, cleaned, sliced
- 3 cups chicken broth
- 1 tablespoon soy sauce

Melt butter in skillet; add onions. Saute until onions are transparent. Add rice and mushrooms to mixture; stir and cook for about 5 minutes. Set aside. Heat chicken broth and soy sauce to boil. Place rice mixture in 1-1/2- to 2- quart casserole; pour broth over all. Stir to mix. Cover with lid; bake at 325° for 1-1/2 hours or until all liquid is absorbed. (May add almonds, if desired.) **Yield:** 8 servings.

HOT BACON DRESSING

Nancy Atherholt, Nazareth, Pennsylvania

(PICTURED ON PAGE 20)

- 4 slices bacon
- 1/2 cup sugar
- 1/2 teaspoon salt, *optional*
- 1 tablespoon cornstarch
- 1 egg, *beaten*
- 1/4 cup vinegar
- 1 cup water
- Fresh spinach leaves, dandelion greens or endive, washed, drained and chilled

Fry bacon until crisp. Remove bacon strips to drain on paper towel; reserve bacon drippings. In small saucepan, combine sugar, salt and cornstarch. Add beaten egg and vinegar; mix well. Add water, crumbled bacon and reserved bacon drippings. Cook to thickness desired. (Extra sugar or vinegar may be added to taste.) Serve over greens. **Yield:** 1-1/2 cups dressing.

CREOLE CORN MUFFINS

Alice Mathews, Alexandria, Louisiana

(PICTURED ON PAGE 20)

- 2 eggs, beaten
- 1-1/2 cups milk
- 3/4 cup shortening, melted
- 2-1/2 cups flour
- 1 teaspoon salt
- 2 tablespoons baking powder
- 4 tablespoons (heaping) sugar
- 4-1/2 tablespoons (heaping) yellow cornmeal
- 2 tablespoons chopped green pepper
- 2 tablespoons chopped onion
- 2 tablespoons chopped pimiento
- 3/4 cup grated cheddar cheese

Blend eggs, milk and shortening together. Set aside. Combine flour, salt, baking powder, sugar and cornmeal in mixing bowl. Add green pepper, onion, pimiento and cheese to cornmeal mixture. Pour milk mixture into cornmeal mixture, stirring just until mixed. Pour batter into *hot* greased muffin pans, 2/3 full. Bake at 400° for 25-30 minutes. **Yield:** 9-12 muffins.

MICHIGAN BEAN BAKE

Sondra Bergy, Lowell, Michigan

(PICTURED ON PAGE 20)

- 1 jar (48 ounces) cooked great Northern beans
- 1-1/2 pounds lean 1-inch pork cubes
- 1/2 teaspoon salt
- 1 bottle (14 ounces) catsup
- 3 tablespoons prepared mustard
- 1-1/2 cups brown sugar
- 1/4 large sweet onion, chopped

Combine all ingredients; mix gently but well. Place in beanpot, casserole or crockpot. Bake at 300°, uncovered, for 5 to 6 hours, cover last hour. OR heat on LOW in crockpot overnight. **Yield:** 10-12 servings.

BIG SKY COUNTRY RIBS & SAUCE

Carolyn Weinberg, Custer, Montana

(PICTURED ON PAGE 21)

- 3 to 4 pounds beef ribs

SAUCE:
- 1 medium onion, minced
- 1 can (10-3/4 ounces) tomato soup
- 1 cup water
- 1/4 cup vinegar
- 1/4 cup Worcestershire sauce
- 1-1/4 cups catsup
- 1/4 teaspoon ground cinnamon
- 1-1/2 teaspoons paprika
- 1/2 teaspoon pepper
- 1-1/2 teaspoons chili powder
- 1/4 teaspoon ground cloves
- 1/8 teaspoon cayenne pepper
- 1 teaspoon A-1 steak sauce
- 1-1/4 tablespoons vegetable oil
- 2 tablespoons brown sugar
- Salt to taste

Brown ribs in broiler pan of oven at 400° for 30-45 minutes. (May do on barbecue grill.) Drain off fat. While ribs are browning, combine all sauce ingredients in saucepan or microwave; simmer for 10 minutes or until flavors are mixed. Cover ribs with sauce. Bake at 300° for 2-3 hours. Baste with sauce as ribs darken. **Yield:** 6-8 servings.

ANADAMA BREAD
Karen Fenley, Greensburg, Indiana

(PICTURED ON PAGE 21)

1-1/2 cups cold OR warm water
1 teaspoon salt
1/3 cup cornmeal
1-1/2 tablespoons butter
1/3 cup dark molasses
1/4 cup warm water
1 package yeast
1 tablespoon sugar
4 to 4-1/2 cups flour, *divided*
Cornmeal for topping

Combine water, salt and cornmeal in saucepan. Stir over medium heat until mixture bubbles and thickens. Add butter and molasses; remove from heat. Cool. In bowl, combine warm water and yeast; sprinkle on sugar. Stir to mix. Add yeast mixture to cooled cornmeal mixture. Add 2 cups flour; beat well. Add 1 additional cup flour; mix. Put 1/2 cup flour on counter; add additional flour as required to knead. Let dough rest; knead again until smooth. Let rise in warm place; punch down. Form into a loaf; place in greased 9- x 5-in. pan. Let rise until dough reaches top of pan. Bake at 375° for 40-45 minutes. Brush top with butter; sprinkle with cornmeal. Return bread to oven for 2 minutes. Cool on wire racks before slicing. (Makes great toast.) **Yield:** 1 large loaf.

BAKED CORN
Jodie McCoy, Tulsa, Oklahoma

(PICTURED ON PAGE 21)

1/2 green pepper, chopped
1/2 onion, chopped
2 tablespoons butter
2 tablespoons flour
1 teaspoon salt
1/4 teaspoon paprika
1/4 teaspoon dry mustard
1 cup milk
1/2 cup dry bread crumbs
1 tablespoon butter
1 beaten egg
2 cups whole kernel corn, canned, frozen or fresh

Brown green pepper and onion in butter for 5 minutes. Add flour, salt, paprika and mustard; stir until blended. Add milk; stir till thick. Brown bread crumbs in 1 tablespoon butter; add crumbs, corn and egg to mixture. Bake in buttered dish at 400° for 30 minutes. **Yield:** 6 servings.

CHOCOLATE WHIPPED CREAM CAKE
Ruth Shelliam, Spring Green, Wisconsin

1 chocolate cake mix
1 pint whipping cream OR 1 8-ounce container of whipped topping
1/3 cup sugar
1/4 cup cocoa

Mix, bake and cook cake according to package instructions using two 9-in. layer pans. Cool completely. Pour whipping cream into chilled mixing bowl. Beat cream, gradually adding sugar and cocoa. Beat until stiff peaks form. Frost and fill cake with whipped cream/cocoa mixture and refrigerate. Let stand in refrigerator for 24 hours before serving. **Yield:** 16-20 servings.

GRANDMA'S HICKORY NUT CAKE
Evelyn Kennell, Roanoke, Illinois

(PICTURED ON PAGE 22)

CAKE:
2 cups sugar
2/3 cup butter
3 eggs
1/8 teaspoon salt
2 teaspoons baking powder
2-1/2 cups flour
1 cup milk
1 teaspoon vanilla
1 cup hickory nuts, chopped (reserve a few halves for garnish)

PENUCHE FROSTING:
1/2 cup butter
1 cup brown sugar
1/4 cup milk OR cream
2 cups confectioners' sugar
1 teaspoon vanilla

Cream together sugar and butter for cake. Add eggs; beat on medium speed of mixer for 2 minutes. Mix dry ingredients together lightly with fork. Add dry ingredients, alternately with milk. Mix well. Stir in vanilla and nuts. Pour into greased and floured 13- x 9-in.

pan. Bake at 325° for 45-50 minutes. (Cake may be baked in 8-in. layer pans.) Cool. Make frosting by melting butter in medium saucepan. Add brown sugar; boil 2 minutes. Add milk; bring to boil. Remove from heat; cool to lukewarm. Beat in sugar and vanilla. (May add chopped hickory nuts, 1/2 cup, if desired.) Frost cake. **Yield:** 16 servings.

LEMON 'N APPLE CHESS PIE
Jodie McCoy, Tulsa, Oklahoma

(PICTURED ON PAGE 22)

FILLING:
1 cup granulated sugar
1/2 teaspoon salt
1/2 teaspoon grated lemon peel
4 eggs, beaten
3 tablespoons lemon juice
1/4 cup butter, melted
1 cup unsweetened applesauce
1 9-inch *unbaked* pie shell

Make filling by combining sugar, salt and lemon peel; set aside. Combine eggs, lemon juice, butter and applesauce. Add dry ingredients to egg mixture; beat with mixer until well-blended. Pour into unbaked pie shell; bake at 450° for 15 minutes. Reduce heat to 350°; bake 15 minutes longer or until set. (May take total of 40 minutes baking time.) Cool on wire rack. **Yield:** 8 servings.

STRAWBERRY CREAM COOKIES
Glenna Aberle, Sabetha, Kansas

1 cup butter
1 cup sugar
1 package (3-ounce) cream cheese
1 tablespoon vanilla
1 egg yolk
2-1/2 cups flour
Strawberry jam

NOTE: Have all ingredients at room temperature.

Cream butter, sugar and cream cheese. Add vanilla and egg yolk; mix. Add flour; blend. Chill dough. Shape into 1-in. balls. Using floured thimble, press hole in center of each cookie; fill with 1/4 teaspoon jam. Bake on ungreased sheet at 350° for 10-12 minutes. **Yield:** 5 dozen.

QUICK TOFFEE BARS
Jeannette Wubbena, Standish, Michigan

12 whole graham crackers,
   broken into quarters
 1 cup butter
1/2 cup sugar
 1 cup chopped nuts
 1 cup semisweet chocolate
   chips

Line a 15- x 10- x 1-in. jelly roll pan with buttered wax paper. Put graham cracker sections on paper. Combine butter and sugar in saucepan. Melt over medium heat; let boil gently 3 minutes. Spoon over graham crackers; spread evenly. Sprinkle nuts on top. Bake at 325° for 10 minutes; cool. Spread melted chocolate chips over all. After chocolate sets, peel off paper. Cookies can be frozen. **Yield:** 48 toffee bars.

MOLASSES CRINKLE COOKIES
Leta Shankel, Heyworth, Illinois

(PICTURED ON PAGE 22)
 1 cup butter
 1 cup *dark* brown sugar,
   well packed
 1 egg
1/4 cup dark molasses (I use
   Gold Label Brer Rabbit
   light, mild-flavored)
1/2 cup nonfat dry milk solids
 2 teaspoons baking soda
1/4 teaspoon salt
1/2 teaspoon ground cloves
 1 teaspoon ground cinnamon
 1 teaspoon ground ginger
1/4 cup wheat germ
2-1/4 cups all-purpose flour

Cream butter and brown sugar until smooth and light. Beat in egg until fluffy. Add molasses and dry milk; beat well. Blend in soda, salt, cloves, cinnamon, ginger and wheat germ; beat 1 minute. Stir in flour until blended. Using 1/3 cup dough for each cookie (or a No. 16 ice cream scoop) form dough into round balls. Roll in granulated sugar; place on well-greased cookie sheet. Sprinkle each with few drops of water. Bake at 375° for 14 minutes. Cool on rack. (Cookies freeze beautifully.) **Yield:** 15 cookies.

FRUIT MUERBETEIG (Custard Kuchen)
L. Jonas, Glendive, Montana

(PICTURED ON PAGE 22)

CRUST:
1/2 cup butter
 1 tablespoon sugar
1/4 teaspoon salt
 1 egg yolk, beaten
 1 cup flour

FILLING:
 3 cups fruit (sour cherries
   or rhubarb)
1-1/4 cups sugar
1/4 cup plus 1-1/2
   tablespoons flour

CUSTARD:
 1 egg
1/4 cup cream

Blend all crust ingredients together; press onto bottom and sides of 9-in. cake pan. For filling, combine fruit with sugar and flour; spoon over crust. Make custard by beating together egg and cream; pour over filling. Bake at 350° for 45 minutes. **Yield:** 10 servings.

CHEESE ZUCCHINI CRISPS
Julie Ifft, Fairbury, Illinois

(PICTURED ON PAGE 24)
1/3 cup cornflake crumbs
 2 tablespoons grated
   Parmesan cheese
1/2 teaspoon seasoned salt
Dash garlic powder
 4 small unpeeled zucchini, cut
   in 1/2-inch strips
1/4 cup melted butter

Combine cornflake crumbs, cheese and seasonings; place in plastic bag. Dip zucchini strips in butter then shake in bag of crumbs to coat. Place on baking sheet; bake at 375° for about 10

minutes or until crisp. **Yield:** 4 servings. **Diabetic Exchanges:** One serving equals 1 bread, 1 vegetable, 2 fats; also, 209 calories, 546 mg sodium, 37 mg cholesterol, 21 gm carbohydrate, 4 gm protein, 12 gm fat.

Recipe evaluated and rated nutritious by registered dietitian.

CHEESE ZUCCHINI SOUP
Jean Thomas, Loysville, Pennsylvania

(PICTURED ON PAGE 24)
 4 slices bacon
1/2 cup onion, finely chopped
2-1/2 cups zucchini, cut in
   1/4-inch slices
 1 cup water
1/2 teaspoon salt

SOUP BASE:
1/4 cup butter
1/4 cup flour
 1 teaspoon salt
1/4 teaspoon pepper
2-1/2 cups milk
1/2 teaspoon
   Worcestershire sauce
 1 cup (4 ounces) shredded
   mild cheese

Cook bacon until crisp; set aside for garnish. Saute onion in bacon fat until tender. Add zucchini, water and salt. Cover; bring to boil. Reduce heat; simmer for 5 minutes until zucchini is tender. Set aside. Prepare soup base by melting butter in 3-qt. saucepan. Blend in flour, salt and pepper. Remove from heat; stir in milk and Worcestershire sauce. Heat to boiling, stirring constantly. Boil for 1 minute, stirring constantly. Remove from heat; stir in cheese. Add vegetables *with liquid* to soup base. Heat to serving temperature. Garnish with crumbled bacon. **Yield:** about 6 cups.

ZUCCHINI MEATLOAF
Nancy Sheets, Delaware, Ohio

(PICTURED ON PAGE 24)

2 pounds ground beef
2 cups coarsely grated, unpeeled zucchini
1 cup dry Italian-seasoned bread crumbs OR regular bread crumbs + 1 teaspoon Italian seasoning
1/2 cup grated Parmesan cheese
1 tablespoon chopped parsley
1 small onion, finely chopped
2 teaspoons instant beef bouillon OR 2 cubes crushed and dissolved in 1 tablespoon water
1/4 teaspoon salt
1 cup milk
1 large egg, beaten

Combine all ingredients in large bowl; mix thoroughly. Pack into 9- x 5- x 3-in. loaf pan. Bake at 350° for 1-1/4 hours. If desired, garnish with zucchini slices sprinkled with paprika during last 10 minutes of baking. (Leftover loaf, sliced thinly, makes delicious sandwiches.) **Yield: 6-8 servings.**

QUICK ZUCCHINI CAKE
Ann Dudlack, Chicago, Illinois

(PICTURED ON PAGE 25)

1 box yellow cake mix
4 eggs
1/2 cup vegetable oil
1 teaspoon cinnamon
2 cups unpeeled, grated zucchini
1/2 cup raisins
1/2 cup chopped nuts
1 tablespoon vanilla
Confectioners' sugar (optional)

Beat cake mix, eggs, oil, cinnamon and vanilla together in large bowl for 6-7 minutes. Fold in zucchini, raisins and nuts. Grease and flour a 10-in. tube pan, spoon in batter and bake at 350° for 40-50 minutes. Test with toothpick at 40 minutes for doneness; retest at 5-minute intervals. Remove cake from pan; let cool on wire rack. Sprinkle with confectioners' sugar, if desired. **Yield: 16-20 servings.**

ZUCCHINI TIPS

● For quick grated zucchini, place unpeeled zucchini chunks in blender; cover with water and blend at "chop" for a few seconds or until processed. Drain off water; pat zucchini with paper towels and use.

● For a tasty tartar sauce, combine 1/2 cup zucchini relish, 1 cup salad dressing and 2 (or more) tablespoons lemon juice.

● For dried zucchini, wash, peel and grate zucchini; press between layers of paper toweling to remove excess moisture. Spread on dehydrator trays; dry for 8-10 hours. Store in air-tight glass containers or heavy plastic bags.

● For frozen zucchini, shred unpeeled zucchini; drain and pat dry on layers of paper towels. Place 2 cups zucchini in freezer bags; seal tightly. Freeze. Can be used in any recipe calling for shredded zucchini.

ZUCCHINI/GRANOLA COOKIES
Dorothy Dahlin, Minden, Nebraska

(PICTURED ON PAGE 25)

3/4 cup butter, softened
1-1/2 cups brown sugar
1 egg
1 teaspoon vanilla
Grated rind of 1 orange
3 cups grated, unpeeled zucchini
3 to 3-1/2 cups flour
1 teaspoon baking soda
1 teaspoon salt
3 cups granola cereal
1 cup butterscotch OR chocolate chips

Cream butter and sugar in large bowl; add egg, vanilla, orange rind and zucchini. Stir in flour, soda and salt. Add granola; mix. Stir in chips. (Dough will be sticky.) Drop by spoonfuls on greased cookie sheet. Bake at 350° for 12-15 minutes. Cool on rack. **Yield: About 100 cookies.**

ZUCCHINI FUDGE CAKE
Gloria Kleman, Columbus Grove, Ohio

(PICTURED ON PAGE 25)

CAKE:
4 eggs
2-1/4 cups sugar
2 teaspoons vanilla
3/4 cup butter, softened
3 cups all purpose flour
1/2 cup unsweetened cocoa
2 teaspoons baking powder
1 teaspoon baking soda

3/4 teaspoon salt
1 cup buttermilk
3 cups coarsely shredded unpeeled zucchini
1 cup chopped walnuts

CHOCOLATE FROSTING:
1 cup butter, softened
2 pounds confectioners' sugar
1/2 cup unsweetened cocoa
1 tablespoon vanilla
1/2 cup milk

In a large bowl, beat eggs until fluffy. Add sugar gradually; beating until mixture is thick and lemon-colored. Beat in vanilla and butter. Combine flour, cocoa, baking powder, soda and salt; stir 1/2 of dry ingredients into egg mixture. Add buttermilk; mix. Add remaining flour mixture; beat until smooth. Fold in zucchini and nuts. Divide batter into *four* 8- or 9-in. round, greased and floured pans. Bake at 350° for 25-30 minutes or until top springs back when gently pressed. Cool in pans 10 minutes; remove to wire racks and cool completely. Make frosting by combining all ingredients in large bowl; beat until creamy. Frost with chocolate frosting. **Yield: 20 large servings.**

POTATOES AND ZUCCHINI AU GRATIN
Nancy Sheets, Delaware, Ohio

3 cups *cooked,* peeled and sliced potatoes
3 cups sliced zucchini, 1/2-inch slices
2 tablespoons water
3 tablespoons butter
3 tablespoons flour
1 tablespoon instant chicken bouillon OR 3 cubes
1-1/2 cups milk
1 cup shredded mild cheddar cheese
2 tablespoons chopped pimiento
1/2 teaspoon thyme leaves
Canned French fried onions

In medium saucepan, cook zucchini in water 5 minutes or until tender. Drain; set aside. In medium saucepan, melt butter; stir in flour and bouillon. Gradually stir in milk. Cook and stir until bouillon dissolves and sauce thickens. Remove from heat; add cheese, pimiento and thyme. Stir until cheese melts. In 1-1/2-qt. baking dish, layer 1/2 of potatoes, zucchini and sauce. Repeat layers. Bake at 350°, uncovered, 25 minutes or until bubbly. Top with onions; bake 2 minutes longer.

ZUCCHINI PARMESAN BREAD

Mary Webb, Kinsman, Ohio

(PICTURED ON PAGE 25)

- 3 cups all purpose flour
- 1 cup peeled, shredded zucchini (drain on paper towel)
- 1/3 cup sugar
- 3 tablespoons grated Parmesan cheese
- 1/2 teaspoon baking soda
- 1 teaspoon baking powder
- 1 to 1-1/2 teaspoons salt
- 1/3 cup butter
- 1 cup buttermilk
- 2 eggs
- 1 tablespoon grated onion

Mix flour, zucchini, sugar, cheese, baking soda, powder and salt together; set aside. Melt butter; stir into buttermilk. Beat eggs in medium bowl; add butter/buttermilk and onion; stir into flour mixture. (Batter will be thick.) Spread in greased and floured 9- x 5- x 3-in. loaf pan. Bake at 350° for 1 hour. (Use toothpick inserted at center to test for doneness.)

ZUCCHINI LEMON BUTTER

Lena McConnell, Tisdale, Saskatchewan

(PICTURED ON PAGE 25)

- 2 pounds zucchini (large size works well)
- Water
- 1/2 cup butter
- 3 cups sugar
- 3 medium lemons OR 2 large lemons (juice and rind) Juice = 1 cup; rind = 3 tablespoons
- 1 package Certo

Peel, slice and boil zucchini in water to cover until tender. Strain; cool. Mash or puree until smooth. Place in large saucepan; add butter, sugar, lemon juice and rind. Bring to full boil, stirring frequently. Add Certo; boil hard for 2 minutes. Skim off any foam; pack in hot sterilized jars. Seal. Store in refrigerator for short periods of time; in freezer for long-term storage. **Yield:** 6 cups.

BEST ZUCCHINI BARS

Marilyn Stroud, Larsen, Wisconsin

BARS:

- 2 cups sugar
- 1 cup oil
- 3 eggs
- 2 cups flour
- 1 teaspoon cinnamon
- 1 teaspoon salt
- 2 teaspoons baking soda
- 1/4 teaspoon baking powder
- 1 teaspoon vanilla
- 2 cups shredded, ungrated zucchini
- 1 small carrot, shredded
- 3/4 cup rolled oats
- 1 cup chopped hickory nuts OR walnuts

FROSTING:

- 1/2 cup soft butter
- 1/4 teaspoon almond extract
- 2 teaspoons vanilla
- 2-1/2 cups confectioners' sugar
- 1 package (3 ounces) creamed cheese, softened

Beat together sugar, oil and eggs in large bowl or in food processor. Beat in flour, cinnamon, salt, baking soda and powder and vanilla. Beat 1-2 minutes until well mixed. Fold in zucchini, carrot, oats and nuts; mix well. Pour into 15- x 10- x 1-in. pan (jelly roll pan or cookie sheet with sides). Bake at 350° for 15-20 minutes. Make frosting by beating all ingredients together until smooth. Set aside. Cool bars; frost. Cut into bars. **Yield;** 3 dozen.

ITALIAN SAUSAGE AND ZUCCHINI STIR FRY

Mary Ballard, La Crescent, Minnesota

(PICTURED ON PAGE 26)

- 1 pound Italian sausage
- 1/2 cup chopped onions
- 2 cups chopped tomatoes, seeds removed
- 4 cups unpared zucchini, julienne cuts (matchstick) OR coarsely shredded
- 1 teaspoon lemon juice
- 1/4 teaspoon salt
- 1/4 teaspoon Tabasco sauce
- 1/4 teaspoon oregano
- Parmesan cheese

Slice sausage in 1/4-in. slices; brown in wok or large skillet. Add onions when sausage is nearly done. Drain. Add tomatoes, zucchini, lemon juice, salt, Tabasco sauce and oregano. Cook, uncovered, for about 5 minutes, stirring frequently. Remove to serving plate; sprinkle with cheese. Serve with crusty Italian bread. **Yield:** 4 servings.

ZUCCHINI CASSEROLE

Linda Pottinger, Winter Haven, Florida

(PICTURED ON PAGE 26)

- 3 whole chicken breasts, *precooked,* chopped in chunks (3/4-inch) OR 4 cups chopped leftover chicken or turkey
- 6 cups diced unpeeled zucchini
- 1 cup onion, diced
- 1 cup shredded carrots
- 1 can (10-1/2 ounces) cream of chicken soup, *undiluted*
- 1 container (8 ounces) sour cream
- 1/8 teaspoon garlic powder
- 1 package chicken flavor stuffing mix
- 1/2 cup butter
- 1 cup cheddar cheese, grated (optional)

Combine zucchini and onion in medium saucepan, add water to cover and bring to boil. Boil for 5 minutes; drain and cool. Combine carrots, soup, sour cream and garlic powder in large bowl. Add zucchini/onion and chicken; mix. Spread in buttered 13- x 9-in. baking dish. To prepare topping, melt butter in skillet, add bread stuffing and seasoning packet and toss well. Sprinkle stuffing over casserole. Top with cheese, if desired. Bake at 350° for 1 hour or until golden brown. **Yield:** 6-8 servings.

ZUCCHINI IN DILL CREAM SAUCE
Josephine Vanden Heuvel, Hart, Michigan

(PICTURED ON PAGE 26)

- 7 cups unpeeled zucchini, cut in 1-1/2- x 1/4-inch strips
- 1/4 cup onion, finely chopped
- 1/2 cup water
- 1 teaspoon salt
- 1 teaspoon instant chicken bouillon OR 1 cube
- 1/2 teaspoon dried dill weed
- 2 tablespoons butter, melted
- 2 teaspoons sugar
- 1 teaspoon lemon juice
- 2 tablespoons flour
- 1/4 cup sour cream

In medium saucepan, combine zucchini, onion, water, salt, bouillon and dill weed; bring to boil. Add butter, sugar and lemon juice; mix. Remove from heat; *do not drain.* Combine flour and sour cream; stir 1/2 of mixture into hot zucchini. Return to heat, add remaining cream mixture and cook until thickened. **Yield:** 8 servings. **Diabetic Exchanges:** One serving equals 1 vegetable, 1 fat: also 73 calories, 419 mg sodium, 11 mg cholesterol, 8 gm carbohydrate, 2 gm protein, 4 gm fat.

Recipe evaluated and rated nutritious by registered dietitian.

ITALIAN ZUCCHINI SALAD
Ida Wester, Shelbina, Missouri

(PICTURED ON PAGE 26)

- 2 pounds zucchini
- 1/2 cup water
- 2 teaspoons seasoned salt
- 12 large ripe pitted olives
- 2/3 cup olive oil
- 1/2 cup wine vinegar
- 1 teaspoon salt
- 1/2 teaspoon paprika
- 1/2 teaspoon pepper
- 1/2 teaspoon sugar
- 1/4 teaspoon basil leaves
- 1 clove garlic
- 1 avocado
- Pimiento OR red pepper strips

Wash zucchini; cut off ends. Cut into 3/4-in. slices. Combine water and salt; pour over zucchini in saucepan. Cook until tender-crisp. Drain; set aside. Cut olives in quarters; add to zucchini mixture. Combine oil, vinegar, salt, paprika, pepper, sugar and basil. Spear garlic on toothpick; add to dressing.

Pour over zucchini mixture in bowl; stir gently. *Chill overnight.* Remove garlic. Several hours before serving, peel avocado; cut into slices. Add to salad; stir. Garnish with pimiento or red pepper. **Yield:** 12 servings. **Diabetic Exchanges:** One serving equals 1 vegetable, 3 fats; also, 167 calories, 469 mg sodium, 0 cholesterol, 5 gm carbohydrate, 1 gm protein, 17 gm fat.

Recipe evaluated and rated nutritious by registered dietitian

CHEESE-SCALLOPED POTATOES/CARROTS
Josephine Wilkins, Pleasantville, Ohio

- 2 cups boiling water
- 2 teaspoons salt (optional)
- 2 pounds potatoes (5 cups) pared and thinly sliced 1/4 inch thick
- 1-1/2 cups sliced onion
- 5 medium carrots (2 cups) pared, diagonally sliced 1/4 inch thick

CHEESE SAUCE:
- 3 tablespoons butter
- 2 tablespoons flour
- 1 teaspoon salt
- 1/8 teaspoon pepper
- Dash cayenne
- 1-1/2 cups milk
- 1-1/2 cups grated sharp cheddar cheese

Place boiling water and salt in large pan and cook potatoes, onions and carrots, covered, for about 5 minutes or until partially tender. Drain. Make cheese sauce by melting butter in small saucepan. Stir in flour, salt, pepper and cayenne, stirring constantly, about 1 minute. Remove from heat; stir in milk and blend well. Bring mixture to boil over medium heat, stirring until thick and smooth. Add 1 cup cheese; stir until melted. Layer half of vegetables in greased 2-1/2-qt. casserole; top with half of cheese sauce. Repeat layers of vegetables and sauce. Top with remaining cheese. Bake, covered with foil, at 375° for 30 minutes. Foil may be removed for last 10 minutes to brown top. **Yield:** 6 servings. **Diabetic Exchanges:** One serving equals 1 protein, 2 breads, 1 vegetable, 3 fats. (Also, 1,400 mg sodium—690 mg if you eliminate salt in cooking vegetables—134 mg cholesterol, 344 calories.) (This recipe works beautifully in microwave, too!)

REUBEN CASSEROLE
Kitty Monke, Regent, North Dakota

- 1 can (16 ounces) sauerkraut, undrained
- 12 ounces corned beef, canned or sliced, crumbled or torn into small pieces
- 2 cups Swiss cheese, shredded
- 1/2 cup lite mayonnaise
- 1/4 cup Thousand Island dressing
- 2 fresh tomatoes, sliced
- 2 tablespoons melted butter
- 1/4 cup pumpernickel OR rye bread crumbs

Place sauerkraut in 1-1/2-qt. baking dish. Top with a layer of beef, then cheese. Combine both dressings; spread over cheese. Top with tomato slices; set aside. Combine butter and bread crumbs in small bowl; sprinkle over tomato slices. Microwave at 70% power for 12-14 minutes or bake at 350° for 45 minutes. Let stand 5 minutes before serving. **Yield:** 6-8 servings.

MOM'S BROWN STEW
Barbara Pricer, Meadow Valley, California

- 2 pounds beef chuck or flank (cut into 1-1/2-inch cubes and trimmed of fat—*reserve* 1 tablespoon beef fat for browning)
- 1 quart boiling water
- 1 teaspoon lemon juice
- 1 teaspoon Worcestershire sauce
- 1 clove garlic, minced
- 1 onion sliced
- 2 bay leaves
- 1 tablespoon salt
- 1/2 teaspoon paprika
- Dash ground allspice OR cloves
- 1 teaspoon sugar
- 6 carrots
- 2 large potatoes
- 1 pound small white onions
- 3 tablespoons flour
- 1/2 cup cold water

Brown meat in melted fat in heavy Dutch oven. Brown meat until all sides are very dark brown but *not burned.* Add boiling water, lemon juice, Worcestershire sauce, garlic, onion, bay leaves, salt, paprika, spice and sugar. Cover; simmer for 2 hours, adding more water if necessary. Cut potatoes into 2-in. chunks and carrots into 1-in.

diagonal slices; peel onions. Add onions; cook 10 minutes. Add carrots, cook 10 minutes then add potatoes. Cook until potatoes are tender. Remove meat and vegetables to heat-proof casserole; keep hot in oven while thickening stew liquid with flour and water mixture. Bring to boil. Pour hot gravy over meat and vegetables. **Yield:** 8 servings. **Diabetic Exchanges:** One serving equals 3 protein, 1 bread, 1 vegetable, 1 fat. (Also, 995 mg sodium, 103 mg cholesterol, 277 calories.)

MELT-IN-YOUR-MOUTH SAUSAGES
Ilean Schulteiss, Cohocton, New York

      2 pounds Italian sausage
         (sweet, mild or hot)
     48 ounces spaghetti sauce
      1 can (6-ounce) tomato paste
      1 large green pepper, sliced
         thin
      1 large onion, sliced thin
      1 tablespoon grated Parmesan
         cheese
      1 teaspoon parsley flakes OR
         1 tablespoon fresh parsley
      1 cup water

Place sausage in skillet; cover with water. Simmer 10 minutes; drain. Meanwhile, place remaining ingredients in slow cooker; add drained sausage (cut in hot-dog lengths if using sweet sausage—it's shaped in large coil). Cover; cook on LOW 4 hours. Increase temperature to HIGH; cook 1 hour more. Serve in buns or cut sausage into bite-size slices and serve over spaghetti. **Yield:** 8 servings.

HONEY WHOLE GRAIN BREAD
Winifred Ewy, Partridge, Kansas

      3 cups (plus) unbleached flour
      2 packages active dry yeast
  1-1/2 teaspoons salt
      1 cup water
      1 cup cottage cheese
      4 tablespoons butter
    1/2 cup honey
      2 eggs
  2-1/2 cups whole wheat flour
    1/2 cup regular rolled oats
    2/3 cup chopped walnuts OR
         pecans

In large bowl, combine 2 cups unbleached flour with yeast and salt. Heat water, cottage cheese, butter and honey until very warm (120-130°). Add warm liquid and eggs to flour mixture. Mix well. Add whole wheat flour, oats and nuts. Stir in remaining unbleached flour (add more if necessary) and knead until smooth and elastic. Let rise until double. Punch down and place in two greased 5-1/4 x 9-1/4- x 3-in. pans. Let rise about 1 hour. Bake at 350° for 35-40 minutes. Remove from pans onto cooling rack. Brush tops with butter. **Yield:** 2 loaves. **Diabetic Exchanges:** One serving (12 slices/loaf) equals 1-1/2 bread, 1/2 protein, 1 fat; also 174 calories, 183 mg sodium, 29 mg cholesterol, 27 gm carbohydrate.

DATE-NUT PINWHEELS
Nellie Atchison, Epworth, Iowa

DATE-NUT FILLING:
      1 package (8-ounce) dates,
         cut up
    1/2 cup water
    1/2 cup sugar
      1 tablespoon lemon juice
    1/4 cup chopped nuts

COOKIE DOUGH:
      1 cup butter, room
         temperature
      2 cups brown sugar, packed
      2 eggs
      1 tablespoon lemon juice
      1 teaspoon vanilla
      4 cups all-purpose flour, sifted
      1 teaspoon baking soda
      1 teaspoon salt

Mix together all filling ingredients in small saucepan; cook over medium/low heat until dates are soft. Cool; set aside. Make dough by creaming together butter and sugar in large bowl until light and fluffy. Add eggs; beat well. Add lemon juice and vanilla; stir. Sift flour; add baking soda and salt. Sift again. Add to creamed mixture; mix well. (Mixture will be somewhat soft.) Divide dough into 2 portions; place on well-floured surface. Roll each out into rectangles about 1/2 in. thick. Spread evenly with cool date-nut filling. Roll up as for jelly roll. Cover with plastic wrap. Slice 1/8-1/4 in. thick with *sharp* knife. Place on greased cookie sheets. Bake at 400° for about 12 minutes or until golden brown. Cool; store. (These cookies freeze well.) **Yield:** 4-5 dozen.

CHEESY CAULIFLOWER CASSEROLE
Faye Plowman, Cardington, Ohio

      3 cups cauliflower, cut in
         pieces
      1 jar (2 ounces) pimiento
      2 tablespoons chopped green
         pepper
      1 can (8 ounces) sliced water
         chestnuts
      2 hard-cooked eggs, chopped,
         optional
      1 small onion, chopped
      1 cup grated cheddar cheese

SAUCE:
      4 tablespoons butter, melted
      3 tablespoons flour
    1/2 teaspoon salt
    1/4 teaspoon pepper
      2 cups milk
      1 cup American cheese, cubed

TOPPING:
      1 to 2 cups cheese crackers,
         crushed
      3 tablespoons grated
         Parmesan cheese

Layer cauliflower, pimiento, pepper, water chestnuts, egg, if desired, onion and cheese in 2-1/2-qt. casserole. Make sauce by melting butter and stirring in flour and seasonings. Cook and stir 1 minute. Add milk gradually. Add cubed cheese and cook until thickened. Pour over vegetables. Sprinkle topping over all. Bake at 350° for 30 minutes. **Yield:** 12 servings.

CARROT SALAD
Janice Swanson, Galesburg, Illinois

      2 pounds carrots, cut into
         1/3-in.-thick rounds
      1 large onion, diced
      1 large green pepper, diced
      1 10-3/4-ounce can tomato
         soup
      1 cup sugar
    3/4 cup vinegar
      1 cup vegetable oil
      1 teaspoon salt
    1/2 teaspoon ground pepper
      1 teaspoon dry mustard

Bring carrots to boil in salted water; boil 5 minutes. Drain; cool. Add onions and pepper. Combine soup, sugar, vinegar, oil, salt, pepper and mustard. Pour over carrots. Refrigerate 24 hours. **Yield:** 12 servings.

Country Inns

Doe Run Inn

Rt. 3, Box 287, Brandenburg, Ky. 40108, 502/422-2982 or 502/422-2042

Directions: U.S. 31W from Louisville to Hwy. 1638 (at Muldraugh), west 10 miles to Hwy. 448, south 1 mile to inn. (4 miles southeast of Brandenburg).

Schedule: Open year-round except Christmas Eve and Christmas Day. Breakfast, lunch and dinner served daily; dining room hours 7:30 a.m. to 9:00 p.m. Smorgasbord featured Friday evening and Sunday from 11:30 a.m. Wine and beer served Monday through Saturday.

Rates and accommodations: private bath double occupancy $35, single $30; common bath double occupancy $25, single $20. Log cabin on grounds (sleeps 8) $100.

MasterCard accepted.

Hours and rates subject to change. Please call or write.

THE MENU may be limited, but at the Doe Run Inn the food is consistently good, prepared by "cooks, not chefs" who have been at the restaurant for years.

The "Kentucky Fried Chicken" on the menu is the real thing—crisp outside, juicy inside—served with crisp green salad with homemade ranch dressing and small, freshly baked biscuits.

Another notable regional entree is Kentucky Ham, which is specially cured, smoked and aged. It has a distinctive, saltier flavor, and a harder texture than other hams. The ham is served with side dishes of parsley buttered potatoes, green beans and baked apple slices.

A basket of hot and flaky biscuits is served with all dinners.

The most popular dessert at Doe Run Inn is old-fashioned Lemon Chess Pie, which has been made at the inn for 35 years. The innkeepers share that recipe and others below:

OLD-FASHIONED LEMON CHESS PIE

- 2 lemons
- 1/2 cup butter
- 2 cups sugar
- 4 eggs
- 2 unbaked pie crusts

Grate entire peel off the two lemons and squeeze all the juice; set aside. Cream together butter and sugar. Add eggs and beat well. By hand, mix in lemon juice and rind until smooth. Divide mixture into two unbaked pie crusts. Bake at 425° until edges of filling begin to brown (watch carefully!). Reduce oven temperature to 300°. When top of pie begins to brown, turn off oven and open oven door. Leave pie in oven until oven is cool. Makes 2 9-in. pies.

BARBIE'S BARBECUE SAUCE

- 1 gallon chili sauce
- 2-1/2 cups vinegar
- 1 cup Worcestershire sauce
- 4 cups water
- 2 cups brown sugar
- 2 teaspoons MSG *or* seasoned salt
- 4 teaspoons hot sauce
- 4 teaspoons dry mustard
- 1/2 cup margarine
- 1 cup chopped onion
- 1 cup chopped green pepper

Salt to taste
Pepper to taste

Combine all ingredients thoroughly in large kettle. Simmer, uncovered, for 1 hour. **Yield:** About 1-1/2 gallons sauce.

SAUERKRAUT SALAD

- 1 gallon (Number 10 can) sauerkraut, drained
- 4 cups sugar
- 2 cups vegetable oil
- 2 cups vinegar
- 1/2 cup chopped green pepper
- 1 cup canned chopped pimentos

Mix all ingredients together in large bowl; store, covered, in refrigerator. **Yield:** 12 one-cup servings.

THREE BEAN SALAD

- 1 gallon canned green beans
- 1 gallon canned wax beans
- 1 gallon canned dark red kidney beans

DRESSING:
- 5 cups vinegar
- 6 cups sugar
- 4 cups vegetable oil
- 1 cup dried chopped onions

Drain all beans; set aside in large bowl. Mix together dressing ingredients until blended. Pour over beans; stir to combine. Store, covered, in refrigerator. **Yield:** 16 servings.

Best Cook

A GLOWING LETTER nominating Mrs. Faye Moon of Stephenville, Texas, as "Best Cook in the Country" came from Ray Lancaster of the same town:

"This lady is a phenomenal cook! Born and raised in the country, she knows all the secrets of wholesome country cooking, with her life-long collection of great recipes.

"As I write this, my mouth waters just thinking of many of the great dishes she's prepared that I've had the pleasure to enjoy."

When we repeated Ray's praise in a call to Mrs. Moon, her reply brought a chuckle: "He must have been unusually hungry when he wrote that letter!"

But after tasting Mrs. Moon's recipes, it's obvious that Ray knew just what he was talking about. See for yourself:

KING RANCH CHICKEN

- 1 5-pound roasting chicken (5 to 6 cups cooked chicken)
- 1 cup chopped celery
- 1/2 cup onion
- 2 quarts water
- 1 teaspoon salt

- 10 to 12 6-inch corn *or* flour tortillas
- 1-1/2 cups reserved chicken broth
- 1 can (10-3/4 ounces) cream of chicken soup
- 1 can (10-3/4 ounces) cream of mushroom soup
- 1/2 cup whole tomatoes and green chilies
- 1/3 package chili seasoning mix
- 1/2 cup chopped green peppers
- 1/2 pound grated cheese (cheddar, Monterey Jack or Co-Jack)

Combine in 6-qt. Dutch oven, chicken, celery, onion, water and salt. Bring to boil; reduce heat. Cover; simmer for 2 to 2-1/2 hours or until chicken is tender. Remove chicken; strain and reserve broth. Remove meat from bones; chop. Line bottom and sides of 13-in. x 9-in. x 2-in. baking pan with quartered tortillas. Combine broth and soups, stirring in chicken. Spread over tortillas. Combine tomatoes and chili mix in blender, mix. Pour over chicken mixture. Sprinkle with peppers. Bake, uncovered, at 350° for 45-60 minutes or until heated through, adding cheese last 15 minutes of baking time. **Yield:** 8-10 servings.

BAKED CRISPY CHICKEN

MARINADE:
- 2 cups buttermilk
- 1/4 cup lemon juice
- 4 teaspoons Worcestershire sauce
- 1 teaspoon garlic powder
- 2 teaspoons paprika
- 1 to 4 teaspoons seasoned salt
- 1/2 teaspoon black pepper

- 6 to 8 chicken breasts
- 1-3/4 cups dry bread crumbs
- 1/4 cup melted butter

Combine marinade ingredients, stirring to blend. Place chicken breasts in pan; pour marinade over all. Marinate, refrigerated, overnight. Drain thoroughly. Roll in crumbs. Place chicken breasts in baking pan; pour butter over pieces. Bake at 350° for 1 hour, uncovered, for a crispier chicken. (Or for less crisp coating, cover with foil and bake for 45 minutes; remove foil, add 1/4 cup water and bake another 15-20 minutes.) Serve on a warmed platter with fresh parsley and tiny red crab apples. (Pan juices would make a nice gravy base.) **Yield:** 6-8 servings.

CINNAMON CRISPIES

- 2 cups flour
- 1/2 teaspoon baking soda
- 2 teaspoons baking powder
- 1 teaspoon salt
- 2 teaspoons cinnamon
- 2-1/3 cups rolled oats
- 1 cup chopped nuts
- 1 cup plus 2 tablespoons shortening
- 2-1/4 cups sugar
- 2 tablespoons molasses
- 2 teaspoons vanilla
- 2 large eggs

Stir together flour, baking soda, powder, salt, cinnamon and oats; mix in nuts. Set aside. Cream together shortening and sugar until light and fluffy. Add molasses, vanilla and eggs to creamed mixture; beat well. Stir in dry ingredients until blended. Drop from small spoon on ungreased cookie sheets. Press flat with fork, if desired. Bake at 350° for 12-14 minutes (longer baking time yields crunchier cookies). Cool on wire rack. **Yield:** 7 dozen cookies.

TEXAS PECAN PIE

FILLING:
- 3 eggs
- 1/2 cup sugar
- 1 cup light corn syrup
- 1/8 teaspoon salt
- 1 teaspoon vanilla
- 1/4 cup melted butter *or* margarine
- 1 cup chopped pecans
- 1 *unbaked* 9-inch pie crust

Beat eggs slightly with mixer; add sugar and syrup and continue beating. Add salt, vanilla and melted butter to mixture. Place pecans in bottom of pie crust. Add prepared filling to pie shell. Cover edge of crust with foil during the first 15 minutes of baking. Bake at 350° for 50-60 minutes or until the center of the pie shakes slightly when moved.

REGIONAL REFLECTIONS! That's what you'll find on these two pages—recipes as varied and as flavorful as the wonderfully diverse people of this land.

These foods truly represent "a taste of the country", with a handsome Peach and Blueberry Cobbler from Arkansas...a robust Southern Black-Eyed Pea Salad from Texas...a Western-Style Shredded Beef Sandwich from Colorado...and a luscious Blackberry Cake from West Virginia that speaks of a slower, more gentle time.

Foods are as much a part of each region of the country as its scenery. So try a taste of each area by sampling these regional dishes. One bite will convince you—you're tasting *country cooking* at its best!

REGIONAL FAVORITES: Clockwise from lower left—German Potato Salad (Pg. 43); Stuffed Zucchini (Pg. 44); Black-Eyed Pea Salad (Pg. 43); West Virginia Blackberry Cake (Pg. 43); Wyoming Whopper Cookies (Pg. 43); Mile-High Shredded Beef (Pg. 44); Door County Sour Cherry Torte (Pg. 44); Peach Blueberry Cobbler (Pg. 43).

SUMMER PICNICS. Summer in the country means picnics "down by the creek", impromptu cook-outs and family reunions where good cooks have a chance to "show their stuff".

We gathered an ensemble of fish and seafood specialties here —each is a regional favorite, famous in its part of the country.

These coastal treats let you capture the flavor of old-time Scandinavian fishermen's feasts with a Door County Fish Boil, or the fresh spiciness of a Gulf Shrimp Salad. Or, you can savor the simplicity of fresh Pacific fish poached in lemon and fresh herbs...or the sweetness of Atlantic Coast crab in a light souffle.

Taste the *bounty* of this country's rich fresh and saltwater food sources as you enjoy these regional heritage favorites!

OUTDOOR EATING! Clockwise from lower left—Texas Shrimp/Rice Salad (Pg. 45); Maryland Crab Casserole (Pg. 44); Door County Fish Boil (Pg. 45); Steamed Pacific Salmon (Pg. 45).

Meals in Minutes

Recipes from Heidi Herb, Forest Grove, Oregon.

"FAST FOOD" with a flair is at the center of this Meals in Minutes menu —pizza, salad and dessert can be on the table in less than 30 minutes!

French Bread pizza is a flexible way to serve up a favorite flavor. If you don't have French bread, *any* kind of bread you have on hand will do! Try English muffins...sandwich rolls...pita bread ...and pile on any meat or vegetable you want. The pizza sauce is ready in only 7 minutes, but you may want to substitute purchased sauce.

A microwave makes this meal even faster! Soften butter for easy spreading by microwaving at 30% power for 10-50 seconds.

Microwave meat and drain it at the same time! Crumble 1 lb. ground beef or pork sausage into a dishwasher-safe plastic colander. (Make sure it has no metal parts.) Put the colander inside a 2-qt. casserole or a deep bowl, and microwave at HIGH for 4 to 6 minutes, until the meat is no longer pink. Break the meat apart with a fork every 2 minutes.

FRENCH BREAD PIZZA

Large loaf French bread, split in half lengthwise
Butter, softened

PIZZA SAUCE:
- 1 can (6 ounces) tomato paste
- 1 can (8 ounces) tomato sauce
- 1/2 teaspoon garlic powder
- 1/2 teaspoon sweet basil leaves, crumbled
- 1/2 teaspoon oregano leaves, crumbled
- 1 teaspoon dried parsley flakes
- 1/4 cup Parmesan cheese

PIZZA TOPPINGS:
- 12 ounces mozzarella cheese, grated, *divided*
- 1 cup *cooked* ground beef OR pork sausage, pepperoni slices, salami slices
- 1/2 cup chopped green pepper
- 1 cup sliced fresh mushrooms

Lightly butter cut sides of bread and place on cookie sheet; toast under broiler until light golden brown— watch carefully. Prepare sauce by combining all sauce ingredients in small saucepan; simmer on low heat for 5 minutes. *OR use 1-1/2 cups prepared pizza sauce. Spread sauce on cut sides of bread; sprinkle cheese over sauce, reserving 1/2 cup. Spread meat and vegetables evenly over cheese; sprinkle with reserved cheese. Bake at 450° for 10-12 minutes until cheese melts. Cut each length in thirds to serve. Yield: 4-6 servings.

ITALIAN SALAD BOWL

- 1/2 head iceberg lettuce, torn in bite-size pieces
- 1/2 head romaine lettuce, cut in 1-inch slices
- 1 cup fresh zucchini, sliced 1/4 inch thick (optional)
- 3 green onions, finely chopped
- 1 jar (6 ounces) sliced marinated artichoke hearts (reserve marinade)
- 1 cup whole black pitted olives, drained
- 1/4 cup Parmesan cheese (optional)

Mix all ingredients together in salad bowl; sprinkle with salt and pepper. Toss lightly with marinade. Sprinkle with Parmesan cheese, if desired. **Yield:** 4-6 servings.

PURPLE COWS

- 1 quart unsweetened grape juice
- 1 quart vanilla ice cream
- 4 tall glasses

Fill glasses 2/3 full with grape juice. Add two scoops of ice cream to each glass. Serve with iced tea spoons. **Yield:** 4-6 servings.

BRING ON the blueberries...and discover the generous goodness of this versatile fruit!

Because they can be grown from Minnesota to Florida, fresh blueberries are in season from May to September—what a blessing for good cooks everywhere!

Toss a handful of blueberries into the Sunday supper pancakes ...try blueberries in your favorite homemade ice cream recipe or fold the bright beauties into a pretty gelatin salad.

Bake with blueberries for a good-taste bonus—they add color and flavor to muffins, cobblers, crisps, biscuits, cakes and pies.

No matter how you use them, blueberries are bound to please.

PICK OF THE CROP: Clockwise from lower left—Blueberry Almond Crunch (Pg. 46); Blueberry Cheesecake (Pg. 46); Blueberry Bran Muffins (Pg. 47); Blueberry Orange Salad (Pg. 47); Baked Blueberry Pudding Cake with Lemon Sauce (Pg. 46); Fresh Blueberry Cream Pie (Pg. 47); Blueberry Sauce (Pg. 47); Blueberry Scones (Pg. 48).

BEAUTIFUL, bountiful blueberries—they've been called "nature's convenience fruit"...and rightly so.

Blueberries need no pitting, peeling or coring to be enjoyed in a variety of attractive and appetizing ways.

Use bright blueberries to top a fancy filled tart such as our prize-winning Blueberry/Kiwi Flan...or layer them in an old-fashioned custard, cake and fruit dessert called Trifle.

Naturally sweet blueberries add flavor and color to company-best coffee cakes...and make tasty toppings for crepes.

There are so many ways to enjoy this native North American berry—blueberries make summer a real taste treat!

BEST BLUEBERRIES! Blueberry/Kiwi Flan (Pg. 46); Blueberry Peach Trifle (Pg. 48); Blueberry Streusel Coffee Cake (Pg. 48); Blueberry/Lemon Crepes (Pg. 47).

WEST VIRGINIA BLACKBERRY CAKE

Dorothy McComas, Branchland, West Virginia

(PICTURED ON PAGE 36)

CAKE:
- 2 cups sugar
- 1 cup butter
- 4 eggs
- 3 cups all-purpose flour
- 1 teaspoon cloves
- 1 teaspoon nutmeg
- 1 teaspoon cinnamon
- 1 teaspoon baking soda
- 1 teaspoon baking powder
- 1 cup buttermilk
- 1-1/2 cups fresh or *frozen and drained* blackberries OR black raspberries

ICING:
- 1 cup butter
- 1 box (1 pound) confectioners' sugar
- 1 teaspoon vanilla
- 3 tablespoons *cold* coffee

To make cake, cream sugar and butter together; beat eggs and add to creamed mixture. Combine flour, spices, baking soda and powder; stir into creamed mixture alternately with buttermilk. Carefully fold in berries. Bake at 350° in three greased-and-floured 8-in. layer pans for 30 minutes. Cool on wire rack. Frost with icing made by beating all ingredients together until fluffy. (Add more coffee, if necessary.) Spread frosting between cake layers and on sides and top. **Yield:** 16-20 servings.

GERMAN POTATO SALAD

Geralyn Gloe

(PICTURED ON PAGE 36)

- 3 pounds (12 medium) red salad potatoes, scrubbed, boiled, sliced 1/4-in. thick
- 1/4 cup finely diced bacon (2 strips)
- 1/4 cup chopped onion
- 1 tablespoon flour
- 2 teaspoons salt
- 1-1/4 tablespoons sugar
- 1/4 teaspoon pepper
- 2/3 cup cider vinegar
- 1/3 cup water
- 1/2 teaspoon celery seed
- 1/2 cup finely chopped celery
- 3 tablespoons chopped fresh parsley

Cook unpeeled potatoes in enough water to cover until tender. Drain; cool slightly. Slice. Fry bacon in skillet until crisp. Saute onion in bacon/fat for 1 minute. Blend in flour, salt, sugar and pepper. Stir in vinegar and water until mixture is smooth. Cook over low heat for 10 minutes, stirring well. Pour over sliced potatoes; add celery seed, celery and parsley. Mix; serve warm. **Yield:** 6 servings.

BLACK-EYED PEA SALAD

Mrs. Douglas Price, Morgan, Texas

(PICTURED ON PAGE 36)

- 1 can (16-ounces) black-eyed peas, drained
- 1 cup finely chopped celery
- 1/4 cup sweet OR green onion, chopped
- 1/2 cup sweet green pepper, chopped
- 1 medium-sized tomato, chopped
- 2 cups lettuce, cut in long, thin strips
- 1 cup commercial coleslaw dressing

Mix all ingredients together; toss lightly. Serve immediately. **Yield:** 6 servings.

PEACH BLUEBERRY COBBLER

Ramona Banfield, Harrison, Arkansas

(PICTURED ON PAGE 36)

FILLING:
- 2 cups fresh OR frozen peaches, sliced in 1/4-inch slices*
- 1/3 to 1/2 cup sugar
- 4 teaspoons quick-cooking tapioca
- 2 teaspoons fresh lemon juice
- 1 cup fresh OR frozen blueberries

Nutmeg

COBBLER:
- 1 rounded cup all-purpose flour
- 2 tablespoons sugar
- 1-1/2 teaspoons baking powder
- 1/8 teaspoon salt, optional

- 1 teaspoon fresh grated lemon rind
- 1/4 cup butter OR margarine
- 1/2 cup cream OR evaporated milk

*(Can substitute nectarines.) Combine peaches, sugar, tapioca and lemon juice in 1-1/2-qt. baking dish. Sprinkle blueberries over top. Cook in microwave on HIGH for 4-5 minutes (stirring after 3 minutes) or until mixture bubbles and is hot throughout. Sprinkle with nutmeg. Meanwhile, prepare cobbler by mixing flour, sugar, baking powder, salt, if desired, and lemon rind. Add butter/margarine, cutting in with pastry blender until mixture resembles cornmeal. Add cream/milk; stir until dough is moistened and mixed. Drop by tablespoons over hot filling. Dust cobbler with nutmeg. Bake at 400° for 25-30 minutes or until top is golden brown. Serve warm with ice cream. **Yield:** 8 servings.

WYOMING WHOPPER COOKIES

Jamie Hirsh, Powell, Wyoming

(PICTURED ON PAGE 36)

- 2/3 cup butter
- 1-1/4 cups brown sugar
- 3/4 cup granulated sugar
- 3 beaten eggs
- 1-1/2 cups chunky-style peanut butter*
- 6 cups *old-fashioned* oats, *not quick-cooking*
- 2 teaspoons baking soda
- 1-1/2 cups raisins
- 1 package (12-ounces) chocolate chips

(*I use Jif brand peanut butter. If unavailable, use another brand, but add several tablespoons water to mixture.) Melt butter over low heat. Blend in sugars, eggs and peanut butter; mix until smooth. Add oats, soda, raisins and chocolate chips (mixture will be sticky). Drop on greased baking sheet with No. 20 ice cream scoop or large spoon. Flatten slightly. Bake at 350° for about 15 minutes for large cookies, 3-in. diameter. Remove to cooling rack. **Yield:** 2 dozen cookies.

STUFFED ZUCCHINI
Jeanette Mortenson, Albert Lea, Minnesota

(PICTURED ON PAGE 36)

      7 fresh zucchini, 4-6 inches long
    1/2 cup chopped onion
    1/4 cup vegetable oil
    1/2 cup coarsely chopped
        fresh mushrooms
      1 clove garlic, minced
Reserved chopped zucchini
      1 package (3-ounces)
        cream cheese
      1 beaten egg
    1/2 cup Parmesan cheese
    3/4 cup finely chopped
        fresh parsley
    1/4 teaspoon salt
    1/8 teaspoon pepper
Additional Parmesan cheese

Scoop out insides of zucchini (melon baller works great), leaving about 1/4-in. shell. Finely chop zucchini pulp; set aside. Saute onion in oil in large heavy skillet. Add mushrooms, garlic and reserved chopped zucchini; cook over medium heat until most of moisture evaporates. Add cream cheese, eggs, Parmesan cheese, parsley, salt and pepper. Mix well; cook for 10 minutes. Cool filling slightly and fill zucchini shells. Sprinkle with additional Parmesan cheese. Place on jelly roll pans; bake for 30 minutes at 350° until bubbly and golden brown on top. **Yield:** 7 servings.

DOOR COUNTY SOUR CHERRY TORTE
Irene Poehler, Sturgeon Bay, Wisconsin

(PICTURED ON PAGE 37)

CAKE:
      1 cup sugar
      2 tablespoons butter
      1 egg, beaten
      1 cup all-purpose flour
    1/4 teaspoon salt
      1 teaspoon baking soda
      2 cups sour cherries, drained
        (reserve juice for
        sauce below)
    1/2 cup chopped walnuts

CREAM LAYER:
      1 pint whipping cream
      2 tablespoons sugar
      2 teaspoons vanilla

SAUCE:
      1 cup cherry juice
    1/2 cup sugar
      2 tablespoons butter
      1 tablespoon cornstarch

Make cake by creaming sugar, butter and egg together. Add flour, salt and soda; mix. (Batter will be *very stiff*.) Add cherries and nuts to batter. Spread batter in greased 13- x 9-in. baking pan or large spring-form pan. Bake at 350° for 30 minutes (13- x 9-in. pan) OR 1 hour in spring-form. Cool. Prepare cream layer by whipping cream, sugar and vanilla until thick. Spread over cool cake; refrigerate. Cook sauce by combining all ingredients in small pan over medium heat. Cook until thick; cool thoroughly. Spoon over cream layer in decorative pattern. Refrigerate until serving time. **Yield:** 16-20 servings.

BROCCOLI/ CAULIFLOWER SALAD
Marcia Hempfling, Hebron, Kentucky

      1 head cauliflower, broken
        into florets
      1 bunch broccoli, cut into
        bite-size pieces
    1/4 cup onion, chopped
      1 ounce pimiento, drained
      1 can (8-ounce) water
        chestnuts, sliced and
        drained
      1 can (16-ounce) kidney
        beans, drained

DRESSING:
    1/3 cup vinegar
    1/4 cup sugar
    1/2 cup creamy salad dressing
    1/3 cup vegetable oil

TOPPING:
      1 cup sharp cheddar cheese,
        grated
    1/2 cup crumbled bacon bits

Combine cauliflower, broccoli, onion, pimiento, chestnuts and beans in large bowl. Set aside. Dissolve sugar in vinegar; mix well. Add salad dressing and oil; mix. Drizzle dressing over vegetables; chill. Before serving, sprinkle topping of cheese and bacon over vegetables. **Yield:** 8 servings. **Diabetic Exchanges:** one serving equals 2 protein, 2 breads, 2 fats; also 285 mg sodium, 27 mg cholesterol, 382 calories, 31 gm carbohydrate.

MILE HIGH SHREDDED BEEF
Betty Sitzman, Wray, Colorado

(PICTURED ON PAGE 37)

      3 pounds chuck roast OR
        round steak
Vegetable oil
      1 cup chopped onion
    1/2 cup chopped celery
      2 cups beef broth OR bouillon

SAUCE:
Beef broth (1-1/2 cups, reserved from
        cooking beef mixture above)
      1 clove garlic, minced
      1 teaspoon salt
    3/4 cup catsup
      4 tablespoons brown sugar
      2 tablespoons vinegar
      1 teaspoon dry mustard
    1/2 teaspoon chili powder
      3 drops Tabasco
      1 bay leaf
    1/4 teaspoon paprika
    1/4 teaspoon garlic powder
      1 teaspoon Worcestershire
        sauce

Brown beef in hot oil on both sides, adding onion and celery at last minute. Combine beef, vegetables and broth in covered Dutch oven or crock pot. Simmer, covered, 3-4 hours, or until tender. Cool; shred beef, separating into strands. Drain vegetables; combine with beef. RESERVE BROTH; skim off any fat. To make sauce, mix beef, vegetables, reserved 1-1/2 cups beef broth, garlic, salt, catsup, brown sugar, vinegar, mustard, chili powder, Tabasco, bay leaf, paprika, garlic powder and Worcestershire sauce. Simmer all ingredients together until heated thoroughly. *Remove bay leaf.* (This mixture keeps well in crock pot on low heat.) Serve with potato rolls or buns. **Yield:** 8 servings.

MARYLAND CRAB CASSEROLE
Nancy Mahoney, Ellicott City, Maryland

(PICTURED ON PAGE 38)

      1 pound well-picked
        crab meat
      3 beaten eggs
      1 tablespoon fresh parsley
    1/3 cup butter, melted, *divided*
      1 teaspoon salt
Dash black pepper
    1/2 teaspoon Worcestershire
        sauce
    1/2 teaspoon prepared mustard
      1 cup evaporated milk

1 tablespoon minced
green pepper
1/2 cup soft bread crumbs (mix
with 1 to 2 tablespoons of
reserved butter)

Butter sides and bottom of 2-qt. baking dish. Combine crab, eggs, parsley and *all but 2 tablespoons of melted butter,* salt, pepper, Worcestershire sauce, mustard, milk and green pepper. Gently pat into dish. Combine bread crumbs with reserved butter; sprinkle on top. Bake at 350° until brown, about 20 minutes. **Yield:** 4 servings.

DOOR COUNTY FISH BOIL
Linda Anderson, Sister Bay, Wisconsin

(PICTURED ON PAGE 38)

Large kettle with colander (canning kettle works fine)
Water
1/2 cup salt
16 small red potatoes
(1-1/2-inch diameter),
ends trimmed off
16 small white onions, peeled
(1-inch-diameter)
16 chunks (2-inch) whitefish
OR lake trout
Butter
Lemons
1/2 cup kerosene for Boil-Over

Bring water (fill kettle 1/2 full) and salt to boil in large kettle suspended over outdoor fire. *Be sure area surrounding fire is raked clear of burnable material —have water bucket nearby.* Add potatoes; boil for 15 minutes. Add onions; boil for 5 more minutes. Add fish; allow water to return to boil; boil for 5 minutes. Using fireproof gloves, *carefully* dash 1/2 cup kerosene on base of open flame. *Stand back immediately as fire will blaze in order to boil-over water and remove fish residue.* When flames subside, carefully remove colander from kettle. Ladle fish, onions and potatoes on platters with slotted spoon. Serve with melted butter and fresh lemon juice. (Traditional fish boil includes coleslaw, rye bread and cherry pie.) **Yield:** 8 servings.

HAM, SWISS CHEESE POTATO SALAD
Ruth Swift, Portland, Oregon

1-1/2 pounds red salad potatoes
4-1/2 tablespoons white wine OR
3-1/2 teaspoons water *plus*
1 tablespoon more vinegar
3 tablespoons white wine
vinegar OR white vinegar
1/4 cup green onion, chopped
3 tablespoons Dijon mustard
3/4 teaspoon salt
1 teaspoon pepper
1/2 cup vegetable oil
1/4 cup fresh parsley, chopped
3/4 cup cooked ham, finely
chopped
1 cup Swiss cheese, finely
shredded

Scrub potatoes, rinse and boil in jackets until tender. Drain; cool and peel. Cut into 1/2-in. cubes; set aside. Combine wine or water, vinegar, onion, mustard, salt, pepper, oil and parsley in jar. Shake well. Add ham and cheese to the potatoes; pour 2/3 of dressing over potato mixture. Mix until blended. Cover; chill thoroughly. Before serving, stir remaining dressing and add more, if desired. **Yield:** 4 servings.

STRAWBERRY SALAD

1 pint frozen strawberries,
reserve juice
1 package (3-ounce) vanilla
pudding, *not* instant
1 package (3-1/4-ounce)
tapioca pudding, *not* instant
1 package (3-ounce)
strawberry gelatin
2 bananas
2 cups whipped cream or
topping

Pour strawberry juice and/or water into 2-qt. glass measure to make 2 cups liquid. Add puddings and gelatin. MW on HIGH for 5-6 minutes or until mixture thickens and boils. Stir once or twice while cooking; cool. Add strawberries, bananas and whipped cream. **Yield:** 8 servings.

TEXAS SHRIMP/ RICE SALAD
Pam Scales Crew, Orange, Texas

(PICTURED ON PAGE 38)

4-1/2 cups water
1-1/2 pounds unpeeled *small*
shrimp, raw
1-1/2 to 2 cups *cooked* rice
1 can (16-ounces) cut green
beans, drained, OR frozen
beans, cooked, drained
1/2 cup pitted ripe olives, sliced
1/3 cup chopped green onions
1/2 cup commercial Italian
salad dressing
3 tablespoons chili sauce
1/2 teaspoon dried basil leaves
1/4 teaspoon pepper
1/8 teaspoon garlic powder
Curly salad greens

Bring water to boil in large pot; add shrimp and return to boil. Reduce heat; simmer 3-5 minutes. Drain shrimp well; rinse with cold water. Cool shrimp; peel and devein. Combine shrimp, rice, beans, olives and onions; toss well. Combine salad dressing, chili sauce, basil, pepper and garlic powder; mix well. Pour over rice mixture; chill. Serve over salad greens. **Yield:** 6-8 servings.

STEAMED PACIFIC SALMON
Jutta Doening, Kelowna, British Columbia

(PICTURED ON PAGE 38)

1 piece (2 pounds) Pacific
salmon OR halibut (can use
steaks, if desired)
2 tablespoons chopped
fresh basil
1 teaspoon dried or
fresh rosemary
1 teaspoon fresh parsley
3 tablespoons butter
3 to 4 tablespoons fresh
lemon juice (1 large lemon)
Salt
Pepper
Heavy aluminum foil

Place fish on large double sheet of heavy foil. Sprinkle basil, rosemary and parsley over fish. Add butter, dotted evenly over fish. Season with lemon juice, salt and pepper. Seal foil tightly to retain juices. Bake at 375° for 25-30 minutes. Fish is done when flakes easily with fork. Garnish with additional fresh herbs, if desired. **Yield:** 4-6 servings.

BLUEBERRY CHEESECAKE

Janet Southwell, Mahone Bay, Nova Scotia

(PICTURED ON PAGE 40)

CRUST:
- 1 cup graham cracker crumbs
- 3 tablespoons sugar
- 3 tablespoons melted butter

CHEESECAKE:
- 2 packages (8 ounces) cream cheese
- 3/4 cup sugar
- 1/4 cup flour
- 2 eggs
- 1 cup evaporated milk
- 1-1/2 teaspoons vanilla

BLUEBERRY TOPPING:
- 3 cups fresh blueberries
- 1/4 cup water
- 1/4 teaspoon nutmeg
- 1 cup sugar
- 2 teaspoons butter
- 2 tablespoons cornstarch
- 2 tablespoons lemon juice

Make crust by mixing ingredients together until blended. Press into bottom of 9-in. spring-form pan; bake at 325° for 10 minutes. Meanwhile, prepare filling by creaming cheese with electric mixer. Add sugar, flour and eggs (one at a time). Beat until smooth; add evaporated milk and vanilla. Mix until blended. Pour slowly over crust; bake at 325° for 40 minutes. Remove to cooling rack. Prepare filling by combining blueberries, sugar, water and nutmeg; cook until blueberries are tender. Add butter and *cornstarch dissolved in lemon juice.* Cook until mixture thickens, about 2-3 minutes. Cool; spread over cheesecake. Refrigerate until time to serve. **Yield:** 12-16 servings.

BLUEBERRY ALMOND CRUNCH

Loretta Coverdell, Amanda, Ohio

(PICTURED ON PAGE 40)

- 1-1/4 cups all-purpose flour
- 1 cup quick rolled oats
- 3/4 cup brown sugar
- 1/4 teaspoon baking soda
- 1/4 teaspoon baking powder
- 1/4 teaspoon salt
- 1/4 teaspoon cinnamon
- 1/3 cup butter
- 1/4 cup chopped walnuts
- 1 can (21 ounces) blueberry pie filling
- 1/2 teaspoon almond extract

In medium bowl, combine flour, oats, brown sugar, soda, baking powder, salt and cinnamon. Cut in butter with pastry blender until mixture is crumbly. Stir in chopped walnuts. Press 1/2 of mixture in 8- x 8- x 2-in. glass baking dish. Stir almond extract into blueberry filling. Pour filling over crumb mixture; spread to edges. Sprinkle with remaining crumb mixture. Microwave on 70% POWER for 9 minutes. *Rotate dish quarter turn every 3 minutes.* CONVENTIONAL METHOD: Bake at 350° for 30 minutes. Serve warm or cold with ice cream. **Yield:** 9 servings.

BAKED BLUEBERRY PUDDING CAKE

Anna Labarr, Himrod, New York

(PICTURED ON PAGE 41)

PUDDING:
- 2 cups flour
- 1-1/2 cups sugar
- 2 teaspoons baking powder
- 3/4 teaspoon nutmeg
- 1/2 teaspoon salt
- 1/2 teaspoon grated lemon peel
- 3/4 cup butter, softened
- 2 eggs
- 3/4 cup milk
- 2 cups blueberries

LEMON SAUCE:
- 1/2 cup sugar
- 1 tablespoon cornstarch
- 1/4 teaspoon salt
- 1/4 cup cold water
- 3/4 cup boiling water
- 1 egg yolk
- 3 tablespoons lemon juice
- 1 teaspoon grated lemon peel
- 2 tablespoons butter

Make pudding by combining flour, sugar, baking powder, nutmeg, salt and peel in large bowl. Cut in butter with pastry blender until size of small peas. Add eggs and milk; mix on low speed of mixer for 3 minutes. Pour into greased and floured 9- x 9- x 2-in. pan; top with blueberries. Bake at 350° for 1 hour and 10 minutes or until tester inserted in center comes out clean. Make sauce by combining sugar, cornstarch and salt in saucepan. Stir in cold water; mix well. Gradually stir in boiling water; cook and stir over medium heat 10-12 minutes or until clear and quite thick. Blend egg yolk with lemon juice; gradually stir into sauce. Stir in peel and butter. Serve warm pudding with sauce. **Yield:** 9 servings.

BLUEBERRY/KIWI FLAN

Pollie Malone, Ames, Iowa

(PICTURED ON PAGE 42)

CRUST (makes two):
- 1/2 cup granulated sugar
- 1/2 cup confectioners' sugar
- 1/2 cup butter
- 1/2 cup vegetable oil
- 1 egg
- 2 cups *plus 2 tablespoons* flour
- 1/2 teaspoon cream of tartar
- 1/2 teaspoon baking soda
- 1/2 teaspoon vanilla

CREAM CHEESE FILLING:
- 1 package (8 ounces) cream cheese
- 1/3 cup sugar
- 1 teaspoon vanilla

FRUIT LAYER:
- 3 cups washed and drained blueberries
- 2 kiwifruit, peeled and sliced thin

CITRUS GLAZE:
- 1/2 cup water
- 1/2 cup orange juice
- 2 tablespoons lemon juice
- 1/4 cup granulated sugar
- 1 tablespoon cornstarch

Mix crust ingredients together well until blended. (If desired, substitute store-bought refrigerated sugar cookie dough.) Grease two 12-in. pizza pans or tart pans with removable bottoms. Divide dough in pans; flatten with hands, dusting with flour if necessary. Build up a slight rim around edges. Bake at 350° for 10-12 minutes or until crust is golden brown. Cool. Carefully remove one crust to round platter (freeze other crust for later use). Cream together cheese filling ingredients; spread on crust. Spread blueberries and kiwi on top of cheese layer in decorative pattern (other fruits such as strawberries, peaches, pineapple or bananas can be substituted if desired). Refrigerate. Make glaze by combining all ingredients in saucepan; bring to boil. Boil 1 minute; cool. Spread over fruit layer; refrigerate until serving time. **Yield:** 16-20 servings.

KIWIFRUIT:

● Is ripe when slightly soft to the touch. ● Ripens in 3-5 days at room temperature and can be stored in a plastic bag for 2-3 weeks in the refrigerator. ● Is prepared by cutting off both ends, then peeling carefully. ● When fresh contains an enzyme which prevents gelatin from setting—so don't use it in molded gelatin salad. ● Undergoes composition changes when combined with dairy products—so when mixing kiwifruit with ice cream, whipped cream, sour cream or yogurt, serve immediately. ● Is best served in fresh fruit cups...on appetizer trays...with cottage cheese, chicken or tuna salads and cream cheese sandwiches.

FRESH BLUEBERRY CREAM PIE
Pamela Brandt, LaPorte City, Iowa

(PICTURED ON PAGE 41)

- 1 cup dairy sour cream
- 2 tablespoons flour
- 3/4 cup sugar
- 1 teaspoon vanilla
- 1/4 teaspoon salt
- 1 egg, beaten
- 2-1/2 cups fresh blueberries
- 1 *unbaked* 9-inch pastry shell
- 3 tablespoons flour
- 1-1/2 tablespoons butter
- 3 tablespoons chopped pecans OR walnuts

Combine sour cream, flour, sugar, vanilla, salt and egg; beat 5 minutes at medium speed of mixer or until smooth. Fold in blueberries. Pour filling into pastry shell; bake at 400° for 25 minutes. Remove from oven. Combine remaining ingredients, stirring well. Sprinkle over top of pie. Bake 10 more minutes. *Chill before serving.* **Yield:** 8 servings.

BLUEBERRY BRAN MUFFINS
Linda Swanson, Kellerton, Iowa

(PICTURED ON PAGE 40)

- 1-1/2 cups bran cereal
- 1 cup buttermilk
- 1 egg, beaten
- 1/4 cup melted butter
- 1 cup flour
- 1/3 cup brown sugar
- 2 teaspoons baking powder
- 1/2 teaspoon baking soda
- 1/2 teaspoon salt
- 1 cup blueberries

Combine bran cereal and buttermilk;

let stand 3 minutes or until liquid is absorbed. Stir in egg and melted butter; set aside. In another bowl, stir together flour, brown sugar, baking powder, soda and salt. Add bran and milk mixture, all at once, stirring until just moistened. Fold in blueberries. Fill 12 greased muffin cups 2/3 full. Bake at 400° for 20-25 minutes. **Yield:** 1 dozen. **Diabetic Exchanges:** One serving equals 1 bread, 1/2 fruit, 1 fat; also, 140 calories, 337 mg sodium, 33 mg cholesterol, 24 gm carbohydrate, 4 gm protein, 5 gm fat.

Recipe evaluated and rated nutritious by registered dietitian.

BLUEBERRY LEMON CREPES
Marilyn Miller, Niantic, Illinois

(PICTURED ON PAGE 42)

CREPES:
- 1/2 cup biscuit mix
- 1 egg
- 6 tablespoons milk

FILLING:
- 1 package (3 ounces) cream cheese, softened
- 1-1/2 cups half-and-half
- 1 tablespoon lemon juice
- 1 package (3-3/4 ounces) lemon *instant* pudding

TOPPING:
- 1 cup blueberry pie filling

Lightly grease 6- to 7-in. skillet; heat until hot. Beat crepe ingredients together until smooth. For each crepe, pour 2 tablespoons batter into skillet. Quickly rotate skillet until batter covers skillet bottom. Cook each crepe until golden brown; loosen edges with spatula and turn. Cook only until golden brown. Stack crepes with paper towel between them. (Crepes may be made in advance and refrigerated, tightly covered, until needed.) Meanwhile, make filling by beating cheese, half-and-half, lemon juice and *dry* pudding mix on low speed of mixer until well-blended, about 2 minutes. *Refrigerate at least 30 minutes.* Spoon about 2 tablespoons of pudding mixture onto each crepe; roll up. Top with remaining pudding mixture; garnish with blueberry pie filling. **Yield:** 6 servings.

BLUEBERRY ORANGE SALAD
June Herke, Howard, South Dakota

(PICTURED ON PAGE 41)

- 2 cups orange juice
- 1 package (6 ounces) orange-flavored gelatin dessert
- 1/4 cup sugar
- 1 teaspoon grated lemon rind
- 2 cups buttermilk
- 2 cups fresh blueberries
- Curly lettuce leaves

Bring orange juice to boil in saucepan over medium heat. Remove from heat; add gelatin, sugar and lemon rind. Stir until gelatin is dissolved. Chill mixture until it is consistency of unbeaten egg whites. Stir in buttermilk; mix well. Fold in blueberries; pour into oiled 6-cup mold. Refrigerate until set. Unmold on lettuce leaves. **Yield:** 8 servings. **Diabetic Exchanges:** One serving equals 1/4 milk, 2 fruit; also, 179 calories, 148 mg sodium, 1.3 cholesterol, 41 gm carbohydrate, 5 gm protein, .3 gm fat.

Recipe evaluated and rated nutritious by registered dietitian.

BLUEBERRY SAUCE
Nellie Brown, Gravenhurst, Ontario

(PICTURED ON PAGE 41)

- 1/2 cup granulated sugar
- 4 teaspoons cornstarch
- 1/2 to 1 tablespoon fresh gingerroot, grated
- Pinch salt, if desired
- 2/3 cup cold water
- 2 cups fresh blueberries
- 1 tablespoon *fresh* lemon juice

In small saucepan, stir together sugar, cornstarch, gingerroot and salt. Gradually stir in water; cook over medium heat, stirring constantly, until mixture thickens and comes to boil. Stir in blueberries; reduce heat and simmer on low for 5 minutes until berries are tender. Serve immediately, or let cool, cover and refrigerate for up to 3 days. Serve hot over crepes, pound cake or waffles or cold over ice cream. **Yield:** 2 cups sauce.

BLUEBERRY SCONES
Betty Jo Elswick, Priest River, Idaho

(PICTURED ON PAGE 40)
2 teaspoons flour
1 teaspoon cinnamon
1 cup blueberries
1-3/4 cups flour
1 tablespoon baking powder
1/4 cup sugar
1/4 teaspoon salt
1/3 cup butter
2 large eggs
3-4 tablespoons heavy cream OR evaporated milk
2 tablespoons milk
Cinnamon sugar

Mix flour, cinnamon and blueberries together lightly; set aside. Sift flour, baking powder, sugar and salt together; cut in butter. Break eggs into measuring cup; beat with fork. Add enough cream/evaporated milk to make 2/3 cup liquid. Lightly stir egg mixture and berries into dry ingredients. Handle dough as little as possible. Turn dough out onto floured board; divide in two portions. Place on ungreased baking sheet; pat each dough portion into circle 6 in. across and 3/4 in. thick. Cut into six wedges. Brush with milk and cinnamon sugar. Bake at 400° for 15 minutes. **Yield:** 12 servings. **Diabetic Exchanges:** One serving equals 1/2 bread, 1 fruit, 1-1/2 fat; also, 167 calories: 227 mg sodium, 63 mg cholesterol, 23 gm carbohydrate, 4 gm protein, 7 gm fat.

Recipe evaluated and rated nutritious by registered dietitian.

BLUEBERRY STREUSEL COFFEE CAKE
Jane Lechlitner, Elkhart, Indiana

(PICTURED ON PAGE 42)
COFFEE CAKE BATTER:
2-1/3 cups all-purpose flour
1 to 1-1/3 cups sugar
1 teaspoon salt
3/4 cup butter
2 teaspoons baking powder
3/4 cup milk
2 eggs
1 teaspoon vanilla
1 cup fresh OR frozen blueberries

CHEESE FILLING:
1 cup ricotta cheese
1 egg
2 tablespoons sugar

1 tablespoon grated lemon peel
STREUSEL TOPPING:
1 cup reserved crumbs
1/2 cup chopped nuts (*finely chopped almonds work well*)
1/3 cup brown sugar
1 teaspoon cinnamon

To make batter, combine flour, sugar and salt in large bowl; cut in butter as for pie crust. *Reserve 1 cup of mixture.* Add baking powder, milk, eggs and vanilla to larger portion of dry ingredients. Beat on medium speed for 2 minutes, scraping bowl constantly. Pour evenly in greased 13- x 9- x 2-in. baking pan. Sprinkle blueberries evenly over batter. Blend cheese, egg, sugar and lemon peel until smooth; spoon evenly over blueberries. Make topping by mixing *reserved crumbs,* nuts, brown sugar and cinnamon. Sprinkle over cheese layer. Bake at 350° for 45-60 minutes or until wooden pick inserted in center comes out clean. Cool slightly before cutting. **Yield:** 20 servings.

BLUEBERRY PEACH TRIFLE
Mary Troyer, Fredericksburg, Ohio

(PICTURED ON PAGE 42)
1 can (14 ounces) sweetened condensed milk
1-1/2 cups cold water
2 teaspoons grated lemon rind
1 package (3-1/2 ounces) *instant* vanilla pudding
2 cups whipping cream, *whipped*
4 cups pound cake, cut in 3/4-inch cubes (*family-size* frozen purchased cake is perfect)
2-1/2 cups fresh peeled and chopped peaches (could substitute nectarines)
2 cups fresh OR dry-pack frozen blueberries, thawed, rinsed and well-drained
Pretty glass bowl, 4-quart size

Combine condensed milk, water and lemon rind in large bowl; mix well. Add pudding mix; beat until well-blended. Chill 5 minutes. Fold in whipped cream. Spoon 2 cups pudding mixture into glass serving bowl; top with 1/2 of cake cubes, all the peaches, 1/2

of remaining pudding mixture, remaining cake cubes, then blueberries and remaining pudding mixture, spread to within 1 in. of edge of bowl. (You want the blueberries to show around the edge of bowl.) Chill at least 4 hours. Garnish, if desired, with a sprig of fresh mint. **Yield:** 20 servings.

CRANBERRY CHUTNEY

1 can (1-pound 4-1/2-ounce) pineapple chunks
2 cups sugar
1 pound fresh cranberries
1 cup white raisins
1/2 teaspoon cinnamon
1/2 teaspoon ginger
1/4 teaspoon allspice
1/4 teaspoon salt
1 cup walnuts, broken

Drain pineapple, reserving juice and fruit. Set fruit aside. Combine pineapple juice, sugar, cranberries, raisins, spices and salt. Cook to boiling; lower heat and simmer for 25 minutes. Add pineapple and nuts. Remove from heat. Store in refrigerator.

BARBECUE BERRY SHORT RIBS
Marietta Peters, Eldridge, Iowa

4 pounds beef chuck short ribs, well-trimmed
2 tablespoons vegetable oil
2 pounds small white onions
2 medium garlic cloves
1 can (8-ounce) whole-berry cranberry sauce
4 large celery stalks, cut in 2-inch pieces
1 cup water
3/4 cup catsup
1 tablespoon prepared horseradish
1-1/4 teaspoons salt
1/4 teaspoon pepper

Heat ribs in oil (few at a time) in 5-qt. Dutch oven over medium heat until well-browned on all sides. Set ribs aside. Reduce heat to medium; add onions and garlic to drippings in Dutch oven and cook until lightly browned, stirring occasionally. Spoon off fat. Return ribs to Dutch oven; stir in cranberry sauce, celery, water, catsup, horseradish, salt and pepper. Cover Dutch oven and bake at 350° for 2-1/2 hours, stirring occasionally. Skim fat off sauce. **Yield:** 8 servings.

CRANBERRY CHEESECAKE
Nairda Monroe, Webberville, Michigan

CRUST:
- 2 cups shortbread cookie crumbs OR graham cracker crumbs
- 1/3 cup melted butter

CRANBERRY TOPPING:
- 1/3 cup water
- 2/3 cup sugar
- 2 cups fresh cranberries
- 1 teaspoon lemon juice

CHEESECAKE:
- 4 packages (8-ounce) cream cheese, softened
- 3/4 to 1 cup sugar
- 5 eggs
- 1 tablespoon lemon juice

Mix crumbs and butter until evenly moist. Press mixture into bottom of 9-in. spring-form pan. Bake at 300° for 5-8 minutes. Cool; reset oven to 350°. Make topping by heating water and sugar in saucepan over medium heat. Bring to boil; boil 1 minute. Stir in berries; cover pan. Reduce heat and cook until most berries have popped, about 3 minutes. Stir in lemon juice. Force topping through sieve or food mill; set aside. Make cheesecake by beating cream cheese in large mixing bowl until light. Gradually beat in sugar; add eggs one at a time. Add lemon juice. Pour into cooled crust. Place 4 tablespoons cranberry sauce on top. Use spatula to cut topping through for a marbled effect. Bake at 350° for 45 minutes. Turn oven off; let sit in oven for 2 hours more. Remove from oven; cool. Pour sauce over top. Refrigerate overnight. **Yield:** 12-16 servings.

CRANBERRY-FILLED ACORN SQUASH
Mrs. Richard Baumbaugh, Greencastle, Pennsylvania

- 1 medium acorn squash
- 1-1/2 cups fresh cranberries
- 6 tablespoons apple juice (divided)
- 6 tablespoons sugar
- 1/4 teaspoon ground nutmeg
- 1/8 teaspoon ground cloves
- 1 teaspoon cornstarch
- 1 tablespoon chopped walnuts

Cut squash in half; remove seeds and large fibers. Cover each half with plastic wrap and microwave on HIGH for 6-9 minutes or until soft. (Rearrange after 4 minutes.) Remove from oven. Combine cranberries, 1/4 cup apple juice, sugar and spices in casserole. Microwave on HIGH 4-6 minutes until cranberries pop. Combine remaining apple juice and cornstarch; mix well. Gradually stir into cranberry mixture; mix well. Microwave on HIGH for 45 seconds to 1-1/2 minutes or until thickened. Spoon cranberry mixture into squash shells; sprinkle with the chopped walnuts. Microwave on HIGH for 1-2 minutes. **Yield:** 4 servings. **Diabetic Exchanges:** One serving equals 1 bread, 1 fruit, 1/2 fat. (Also, 2 mg sodium, 137 calories, 32 gm carbohydrate.)

CRANBERRY CUES

- The peak months for cranberries are September to January. Look for fresh cranberries in ready-to-freeze 12-oz. plastic bags in your produce section. Just toss the bag into your freezer!
- To use frozen cranberries, rinse in cold water; drain. DO NOT THAW.
- Remember that 1 lb. of fresh berries measures 4 cups and yields about 1 qt. of whole-berry or jellied sauce.
- Make frozen cranberry salads in cupcake liners. They're easy to transport to family dinners and stay neat on the dinner plate.
- Put whole cloves in lemon or orange slices to float in hot or cold cranberry drinks.
- Combine any drained cranberry juices and pineapple juice (left over from gelatin salads) as a base for non-alcoholic holiday drinks. Add ginger ale or white soda for a pretty, festive punch.
- When cranberries are in season, make this salad base and freeze in cartons for later use: 1 package (12-oz.) chopped cranberries, 2 whole ground oranges, 2 whole ground apples and 2 cups sugar. Add 2 cups of this base to your favorite red gelatin dessert dissolved in 1-3/4 cups water.

CRANBERRY COLESLAW
Edna McCune, Olds, Alberta

- 1 cup chopped fresh cranberries
- 1/4 cup sugar
- 3 cups finely shredded cabbage
- 1/2 cup orange juice
- 2 tablespoons chopped celery
- 2 tablespoons chopped green pepper
- 1 cup seeded green grapes, halved

DRESSING:
- 2 tablespoons mayonnaise OR salad dressing
- 2 tablespoons plain yogurt

Combine cranberries and sugar; set aside. Moisten cabbage with orange juice. Add cranberry/sugar mixture, celery, green pepper and grapes. Combine dressing ingredients. Toss salad with dressing. Chill at least 1/2 hour before serving. **Yield:** 8 servings. **Diabetic Exchanges:** One serving equals 1 vegetable, 1 fruit, 1/2 fat. (Also, 34 mg sodium, 3 mg cholesterol, 86 calories, 15 gm carbohydrate.)

WALNUT CRANBERRY RELISH
Mary Ungs, New Vienna, Iowa

- 1 pound fresh cranberries
- 1-1/2 cups sugar
- 1 cup coarsely chopped walnuts
- 1 cup orange marmalade
- Juice of 1 lemon OR lime (about 3 tablespoons)

Rinse cranberries; drain. Place in shallow baking pan with sugar; mix well. Cover pan with foil. Bake at 350° for 1 hour. Meanwhile, spread walnuts in shallow baking pan. Place in oven with cranberries for about 10 minutes, until lightly toasted. Combine baked cranberries, nuts, marmalade and lemon/lime juice in medium bowl; mix well. Refrigerate, covered, until well-chilled (at least 6 hours). **Yield:** 4 cups or 8-10 servings.

SPICED CRANBERRIES
Clara Olivers, Kent, Washington

- 2 quarts fresh cranberries
- 1-1/2 cups vinegar
- 2/3 cup water
- 6 cups sugar
- 2 tablespoons cinnamon
- 1 tablespoon ground cloves
- 1 tablespoon ground allspice

Combine all ingredients in large saucepan and boil gently for 45 minutes. Put up mixture in hot sterilized jars. Cover and store in refrigerator. **Yield:** 3 pints.

Country Inns

Parish Patch Farm & Inn
Normandy, Tennessee 37360, 615/857-3441

Directions: From Nashville take I-24 south to Exit 97. Turn right onto Hwy. 64 West to Wartrace. In Wartrace, take Hwy. 269 East 4 miles to inn.

Schedule: Open year-round except on Christmas Day. Full breakfast included for inn guests. Dinner served by reservation at additional cost.

Rates: 6 rooms with private baths, $60 to $85; 2 cottages, $110; 1 apartment, $100; bunk room with 7 twin beds, $25 per bed. These rates are for double occupancy, except bunk room. Charge for extra person: $10. No pets.

Visa and MasterCard are accepted.

Hours and rates subject to change. Please call or write.

FRESH ingredients and Southern country cuisine are the rule at Parish Patch Farm & Inn. Add the welcoming touches of Southern hospitality —fresh flowers and flowering plants …pumpkin bread to welcome you shortly after arrival…helping guests plan a tour of the area—and you see what makes this inn special.

The full breakfast included in the room rates is a hearty, Southern-style country meal—scrambled eggs, pork sausage, grits, biscuits with homemade jam, orange juice and coffee—served on a pretty porch attached to the dining room.

Dinner may be enjoyed either in the luxurious comfort of the inn's dining room or at the inn's historic Cortner Mill restaurant on another part of the grounds.

In either dining room, the cuisine is the true treat, though. A typical dinner includes fresh spinach salad with hard-boiled eggs and sliced mushrooms, mini-loaves of home- made wheat bread, buttermilk-pecan chicken breasts, stuffed zucchini and "Sawdust Pie" for dessert. The recipe for this rich and delicious dessert is provided below.

PARISH PATCH SAWDUST PIE

1-1/2 cups coconut
1-1/2 cups graham cracker crumbs
1-1/2 cups pecans, chopped
1-1/2 cups sugar
1 cup egg whites, *unbeaten*
1 unbaked pie crust

Combine coconut, graham cracker crumbs, pecans and sugar. Mix with egg whites. Pour mixture into pie shell. Bake at 350° for 35 minutes.

Kay El Bar Guest Ranch
P.O. Box 2480, Wickenburg, Arizona 85358, 602/684-7593

Directions: U.S. 60/89 northwest from Phoenix to Wickenburg, north on 89/93 to Rincon Road and follow the signs.

Schedule: Open from October 15 to May 1 (give or take a few days). Two nights minimum stay, 4 nights minimum during the holidays.

Accommodations: Eight rooms in main lodge, all with private baths; two-bedroom, two-bath guest cottage with living room and fireplace.

Rates: Lodge—one person $80 daily, two persons $145, children (in same room as parents) 2-6 years $25, 7-12 years $40. Cottage—two persons $165, four persons $295, extra person $55. Weekly, monthly and special group rates available. MasterCard and Visa accepted.

Hours and rates subject to change. Please call or write.

MEALS at the Kay El Bar Guest Ranch range from cookout break- fasts and sack lunches on the trail to crab-stuffed fish with rice pilaf on a Friday evening. After enjoying such before-dinner refreshment as a big, round loaf of rye bread hollowed out and filled with spinach dip, it's on to dinner in the ranch dining room.

Dinners vary according to what's fresh and looks good. The cooks have a free rein on menus, with the one standard meal being the steaks fried outdoors over a mesquite fire on Saturday night. On a Friday night, dinner could consist of baked, crab-stuffed fish, brown and wild rice pilaf, crisp-cooked broccoli and cornbread, with a dessert of lemon pie, crowned with a high meringue.

The Kay El Bar's popular recipe for Corn Relish is shown at right— try it to add a tangy, Western-style touch to one of your meals soon!

KAY EL BAR CORN RELISH

1 cup salad oil
1/2 cup plus 2 tablespoons vinegar
1-1/4 teaspoons lemon juice
1/4 cup chopped parsley
3-1/2 teaspoons salt
1/2 cup sugar
1-1/4 teaspoons leaf basil
5 tomatoes, peeled and chopped
1-1/4 cups green pepper, chopped
1-1/2 cups green onion, chopped
5 cups kernel corn

Mix ingredients well. Refrigerate for several hours, allowing flavors to mix.

CREATING and re-creating recipes is a big part of what makes Jim Johnson of Atchison, Kansas the "Best Cook in the Country", according to his wife, Linda, who nominated him for the honor.

"Jim loves to go into the kitchen and experiment, taking my 'good ol' recipes' and adding a bit-of-this and a shake-of-that to see what happens. I'm sometimes skeptical, but often he improves the recipe!

"He loves to come home and re-create something we've tried in a restaurant, too. It may take several tries, but in the end Jim figures out the recipe—sometimes it's better than the original," Linda wrote.

"When we got married, Jim didn't know how to cook, but it didn't take him long to learn—and now he loves it. He often takes a recipe from a magazine or newspaper and disappears into the kitchen 'just to try it'.

"Jim also has great patience when it comes to teaching our girls how to cook (more than I do). One of my greatest joys is to listen to them in the kitchen 'creating'. I'm sure the girls will have happy memories of cooking with their dad.

"Another quality that makes Jim a good cook is that he cleans up the kitchen when he is done creating. When we're both cooking, he will even clean up *my* messes. How can you beat that?"

NEW ENGLAND VEGETABLES

1 package (10 ounces) frozen, chopped broccoli
1/2 cup butter
1 tablespoon cornstarch
1 can (12 ounces) Mexicali corn, drained
1 can (16 ounces) French-cut green beans, drained
1/4 teaspoon garlic salt
1 tablespoon Parmesan cheese

Cook broccoli according to package directions, drain; set aside. In 2 qt. glass casserole, melt butter in microwave on HIGH 30-60 seconds. Stir in cornstarch; microwave on HIGH an additional 1-2 minutes, stirring every 30

seconds until butter is slightly thickened. Add vegetables, including reserved broccoli, garlic salt and Parmesan cheese. Heat on HIGH in microwave 5 minutes, stirring twice or until vegetables are hot. **Yield:** 8 servings.

HOT SPICED CIDER

1 quart apple cider
1 cup orange juice
1/2 cup pineapple juice
1/2 cup lemon juice
1/2 cup sugar
2 2-inch sticks cinnamon
1 teaspoon whole cloves

Combine all ingredients in 2 quart microwaveable pitcher. Microwave on HIGH 10 minutes; let cider stand 5 minutes. Microwave on HIGH an additional 3-4 minutes. **Yield:** 6-8 servings.

MARDI GRAS RICE

2/3 cup raw long grain rice
12 ounces bacon
1/2 cup green onions, sliced
1 pint canned tomatoes, chopped and drained
1/4 teaspoon leaf thyme
1-1/2 cups shredded cheddar cheese

Cook rice in heavy saucepan in 1 2/3 cups water and 1/2 teaspoon salt. Drain; set aside. Fry bacon; crumble and set aside, reserving 2 tablespoons bacon drippings. Saute onions in bacon drippings until onions are soft. In 1-1/2 qt. casserole, combine the cooked rice, bacon, onions, tomatoes, thyme and cheese; mix well. Cover; bake at 350° for 25 minutes. **Yield:** 6 servings.

HUSHPUPPIES

1-3/4 cups biscuit mix
3/4 cup yellow cornmeal
1/2 teaspoon salt
1 teaspoon baking powder
1/4 cup dried onion flakes
1 tablespoon sugar
1 cup milk
Oil for deep fat frying

Combine all dry ingredients in bowl; add milk, stirring until mixed. Drop by spoonfuls into hot oil. (Form by shaping into walnut-sized balls but be advised that equal amounts of biscuit mix and cornmeal may have to be added to reduce stickiness of batter.) Deep fry until golden brown, turning once. **Yield:** About 40 hushpuppies.

CHOCOLATE

● Don't overcook chocolate. Remove it from the heat before it's completely melted. ● When you melt chocolate by itself, the container and utensil must be *absolutely* dry. If not the chocolate may "stiffen" (harden) and turn grainy. ● If chocolate should stiffen while melting, you can salvage it by adding solid shortening (Crisco)—1 teaspoon for each ounce of chocolate. ● Cocoa may be used in place of baking chocolate. Three tablespoons of cocoa plus 1 tablespoon of shortening or oil equals 1 square (1 ounce) of baking chocolate. ● To make chocolate rose leaves for garnishing desserts, cut, wash and thoroughly dry fresh leaves. Melt 2 oz. semi-sweet chocolate or milk chocolate with 2 oz. bitter chocolate in top half of double boiler. *(Do not get any water in chocolate.)* When chocolate's smooth and easy to stir, paint (with small brush) onto back of leaf, *staying away from the edges.* Add repeated coatings until thickness of 1/16 in. is reached. Chill, chocolate side up, on foil lined tray. Carefully peel away leaf. Cover and refrigerate until ready to use. (Use within 1-2 weeks.)

BLUE RIBBON FOOD! Won't you sample crisp Country-Fried Chicken from Indiana, Stuffed and Scalloped Potatoes from Idaho, spicy grilled beef Fajitas from Texas and colorful fresh Salsa from California?

Leave room to taste tender brown sugar-glazed Ham Balls and traditional Amish sweet-and sour relishes and salads.

These are the recipes that win blue ribbons at state and county fairs—and warm praise at America's tables.

Why not give these tried-and-true classics a try today and enjoy a *real* taste of the country?

PRIZE-WINNING RECIPES: Clockwise from lower left—Country Fried Chicken (Pg. 59); Corn Relish (Pg. 59); Ham Balls (Pg. 59); Idaho Dutch Scalloped Potatoes (Pg. 60); Nine-Day Coleslaw (Pg. 60); Fresh California Salsa (Pg. 60); Shrimp-Stuffed Potatoes (Pg. 59); Fajitas (Pg. 59).

BEST OF SHOW! Delicious dessert dishes showcasing juicy golden peaches, flavorful cooking apples and tart-and-sweet Concord grapes take the blue ribbon here. And a classic pound cake is the perfect accompaniment for any fresh fruit.

Taste the best of Wisconsin's dairyland in the lightly spiced Apple/Cheese bars; the fruit-filled goodness of East Coast vineyards in Harvest Grape Pie; and the smooth delicacy of Southern peaches in Praline Pie or heaped on the light, rich Pound Cake.

Sweet treats to savor—these are award-winning recipes from across America's great countryside!

JUDGES' FAVORITES! Clockwise from lower left—Harvest Grape Pie (Pg. 60); Apple/Cheese Bars (Pg. 60); Pound Cake (Pg. 61); Peach Praline Pie (Pg. 61).

Meals in Minutes

Recipes from Karen Ann Bland, Gove, Kansas.

THIRTY MINUTES from start to finish—and hearty and delicious as well! Serve up this tasty meal in less than half an hour, then sit back and listen to the appreciative comments!

Make the no-bake granola-style cookies first, then chill them as you fix the rest of the meal. (HINT: The salad is an old-time standby that's ideal for children to assemble with just a little guidance.)

As the pasta simmers, cut and cook the remaining main-dish ingredients. (You'll notice this recipe is a great way to use up summer garden vegetables.) There's even time to make a pot of coffee and pour the milk before your half-an-hour's up!

You can accompany this meal with sliced French bread as pictured, or, if you have a supply of Quick Bread Sticks on hand, serve those crunchy, herb-savory treats instead!

MICROWAVE TIME-SAVER: To defrost frozen orange juice concentrate, remove lid and put *cardboard* container in oven. Microwave on HIGH for 15-30 seconds.

JUICE TIP: To get more juice from lemons and oranges, microwave on HIGH for 30 seconds per fruit before squeezing.

CONFETTI SPAGHETTI

- 1 cup pepperoni slices OR 1 package (4 ounces)
- 1/2 cup chopped onion
- 1/2 cup green pepper strips
- 7 ounces spaghetti, *cooked and drained*
- 1/2 cup grated Parmesan cheese
- 1/2 cup (2 ounces) shredded mozzarella cheese
- 1/2 cup chopped tomato
- 1/2 teaspoon oregano leaves

Fry the pepperoni in large skillet until edges curl. Add onion and green pepper; cook until tender. Toss together cooked spaghetti and cheeses, tomato and oregano; add pepperoni, onions and pepper strips. Heat thoroughly. Sprinkle with additional Parmesan cheese, if desired. **Yield:** 4-6 servings.

PEAR/LETTUCE SALAD

- 8 canned pear halves, drained
- 8 large lettuce leaves
- Non-dairy whipped topping
- 4 teaspoons shredded cheddar cheese

For each salad, first arrange 2 lettuce leaves on plate; top with 2 pear halves, hollow side up. Fill each pear cavity with a spoonful of topping. Sprinkle each salad with 1 teaspoon cheese. Chill until serving time. **Yield:** 4 servings.

NO-BAKE ORANGE PEANUT BUTTER DROPS

- 3/4 cup sugar
- 1/4 cup frozen orange juice concentrate, thawed
- 1/4 cup butter
- 1/4 cup crunchy peanut butter
- 1-1/2 cups quick-cooking oats
- 1/2 cup raisins

Using medium-size saucepan over medium heat, combine sugar, orange juice concentrate and butter, stirring constantly until mixture boils. Remove from heat; stir in peanut butter until blended. Add oats and raisins; stir to blend. Drop by teaspoonsful onto waxed paper. Chill until firm. **Yield:** 30 cookies (1-1/2 inches each).

QUICK BREAD STICKS

- 12 day-old hot dog buns
- 1 cup butter, softened
- 1 teaspoon sweet basil leaves, crushed
- 1 teaspoon dried dill weed
- 1/4 teaspoon garlic powder

Quarter buns (lengthwise). Combine remaining ingredients in small bowl; mix. Spread butter/herb mixture on cut sides of buns. Place on two cookie sheets or jelly roll pans. Bake at 250° for 1 hour to 1-1/2 hours or until crisp. **Yield:** 48. **Diabetic Exchanges:** One serving equals 1/2 bread, 1 fat; also, 64 calories, 97 mg sodium, 12 mg cholesterol, 5 gm carbohydrate.

BECAUSE onions and their cousins are available year-round, they are among our most widely used seasonings.

Uncover an omelet, and you'll find green onions tucked inside... sizzle a bright stir-fry dish or simmer a tasty soup, and you'll discover more delicious evidence. Bite into a tender brown oatmeal bun, and a sensational combination of onion and crisp bacon bits will greet you.

Onions also appear to good-tasting advantage in cold, marinated salads and in warm, fresh-from-the-oven kuchen appetizers.

No matter how you slice them, you'll find a lot to like about onions and their zesty relatives.

ALL ONION: Clockwise from lower left—Onions and Stir-Fry Beef (Pg. 61); Onion Bread Kuchen (Pg. 61); Onion/Bacon Oatmeal Buns (Pg. 61); Hammerlock Onions (Pg. 62); Green Onion Omelet (Pg. 62); French Onion Casserole (Pg. 62); Chicken with 40 Cloves of Garlic (Pg. 62); Russian Leek Soup (Pg. 62).

ONLY ONIONS can fill the flavor gap in so many foods! Sweet or pungent, mild or strong, onions (and their cooking cousins—chives, garlic, leeks and shallots) can work wonders in the kitchen. Onions can make a bland gravy grand ...save a sauce...salvage a soup ...or stand alone in a hearty casserole.

However you use onions, make them a frequent feature of your family's meals. They will put a tasty new tang on your table!

ORIGINAL ONIONS: Onion Italian Sausage (Pg. 63); Cream of Leek Soup (Pg. 63); Garlic Roasted Potatoes (Pg. 63); Baked Onions with Dill (Pg. 62).

COUNTRY FRIED CHICKEN
Edna Hoffman, Hebron, Indiana

(PICTURED ON PAGE 52)

1 fryer chicken (3 pounds) or equivalent pieces
3/4 to 1 cup buttermilk

COATING:
1-1/2 to 2 cups flour
1-1/2 teaspoons salt
1/2 teaspoon pepper
1/2 teaspoon garlic powder
1/2 teaspoon onion powder
1 tablespoon paprika
1/4 teaspoon ground sage
1/4 teaspoon ground thyme
1/8 teaspoon baking powder
Sunflower Oil for frying

Wash and pat dry chicken pieces with paper towel; place in large flat dish. Pour buttermilk over chicken; cover, and allow to soak at least one hour or overnight in refrigerator. Combine coating ingredients in double strength paper bag and shake chicken pieces, *one at a time,* to coat well. Lay coated pieces on wax paper on counter for 15 minutes to allow coating to dry (will cling better in frying). Meanwhile pour oil to depth of 1/2 inch in electric skillet and heat to 350-360°. Fry chicken, several pieces at a time, for about 3 minutes on each side. Be careful not to over-crowd. Reduce heat to 320°, cook chicken, turning occasionally, for 25-35 minutes or until juices run clear and chicken is tender. Remove to paper towel-lined platter. **Yield:** 4 servings.

CORN RELISH
Lucy Zimmerman, Ephrata, Pennsylvania

(PICTURED ON PAGE 52)

6 pints sweet corn, cut from cobs
4 bell peppers, red and green, seeded and diced
3 onions, diced
1 head celery, diced
2 cups granulated sugar
1 pint vinegar
2 tablespoons salt
1 teaspoon mustard seed
1 pint water

Combine all ingredients in large non-aluminum kettle; bring to a boil. Reduce heat; simmer, uncovered, until vegetables are tender, about 30-40 minutes. Pack into hot, sterilized jars, leaving 1/2-inch headspace. Seal. Cool completely. Store in refrigerator or for long-term storage in the freezer for up to 1 year. **Yield:** 9 pints.

HAM BALLS WITH MUSTARD SAUCE
Ardath Murray, Bartlesville, Oklahoma

(PICTURED ON PAGE 52)

1-1/4 pounds ground ham
2/3 pound ground fresh pork
2/3 pound ground beef
2 eggs
1 cup tomato juice
2 tablespoons minced onion
1 cup cracker crumbs
1/2 teaspoon salt
2 tablespoons green pepper

SAUCE:
1 cup brown sugar
1/2 cup vinegar
1/2 cup water
2 teaspoons dry mustard

Combine ham, pork and beef; add eggs, juice, cracker crumbs, onion, green pepper and salt. Shape into golf-ball size balls; place in flat baking dish and bake at 350° for 1 hour. Meanwhile make sauce by dissolving brown sugar, vinegar, water and dry mustard in pan. Pour over ham balls after they have baked 1 hour. Bake 30 minutes longer. **Yield:** 8 servings.

FAJITAS
Mrs. Richard Moore, Brownsville, Texas

(PICTURED ON PAGE 53)

2-1/2 pounds trimmed beef skirt, flank steak or beef rib meat (boned)

MARINADE:
1 fresh lime
12 ounces beer
1 cup Italian dressing
Teriyaki Baste and Glaze
12 flour tortillas

PICO DE GALLO:
1 large tomato, chopped
1 large green pepper, chopped
1 onion, chopped

Remove any skin and fat from beef skirt or other cut of beef. Combine juice of 1 lime, beer and dressing. Place beef in flat pan; pour marinade over all. Allow to marinate for 2-3 hours. Drain beef; place on hot grill and cook, turning once, about 5 minutes, depending on thickness. Brush with teriyaki glaze. Slice thin, on a diagonal, and place in warm flour tortillas with several tablespoons of Pico De Gallo (tomato, green pepper and onion which have been combined). Fold tortillas to enclose meat and vegetables. Serve with Picante sauce, if desired. **Yield:** 6 servings.

SHRIMP-STUFFED POTATOES
Aney Chatterton, Soda Springs, Idaho

(PICTURED ON PAGE 53)

6 medium baking potatoes
1/2 cup butter OR margarine
1 cup grated sharp cheddar cheese
1 teaspoon salt
Dash cayenne pepper
2 tablespoons onion, minced
3/4 cup milk
1 can (4-1/2 ounces) broken or tiny shrimp
Paprika
Fresh parsley

Scrub potatoes well; prick with fork. Bake at 400° for 1 hour or until done. Cut potatoes in half lengthwise; scoop out pulp, leaving enough to keep potatoes shape. Set skins aside. Combine pulp with butter, cheese, salt, pepper, onion and milk. Whip with electric mixer until smooth and fluffy. Fold in shrimp. Refill potato shells. Sprinkle tops with paprika and parsley. Bake at 375° for 15-20 minutes or microwave at 50% POWER until hot. **Yield:** 6 servings.

NANA'S DEVILED EGGS
Carol Mersberger, Lynden, Washington

12 eggs, hard-cooked, cooled

FILLING:
Mashed yolks
  1/4 cup melted butter
    2 teaspoons sweet pickle juice
    2 tablespoons prepared mustard
    1 tablespoon Worcestershire sauce
  1/4 teaspoon dill weed
  1/4 cup real bacon bits
Salt and pepper to taste
  1/2 cup creamy salad dressing
Paprika

Peel eggs; cut in half. Remove yolks; mash with fork. Add all filling ingredients to yolks; mix until smooth. Refill whites; sprinkle with paprika. **Yield:** 12 servings.

EGG TRIVIA:
● Hard-cooked eggs spin easily; raw eggs won't.
● Hard-cooked eggs keep up to 10 days in the refrigerator. But don't leave them out. Bacteria can enter through the eggshell.
● Brown- and white-shelled eggs have the same nutritional value.

NINE-DAY COLESLAW
Ardath Murray, Bartlesville, Oklahoma

(PICTURED ON PAGE 53)

DRESSING:
    1 cup vinegar
  1/2 cup vegetable oil
    2 teaspoons celery seed
    2 teaspoons granulated sugar
  1/2 teaspoon salt

COLESLAW:
    3 pounds cabbage, shredded
    1 cup onion, finely chopped
  1/2 cup green pepper, finely chopped
  1/2 cup red pepper, finely chopped
    2 cups granulated sugar

Combine dressing ingredients in saucepan; bring to boil. Cool; set aside. Combine cabbage, onion, peppers and sugar. Let stand until sugar dissolves. Pour cooled dressing over cabbage mixture; refrigerate. This coleslaw keeps well under refrigeration. **Yield:** 2 quarts.

IDAHO DUTCH SCALLOPED POTATOES
Gladys De Boer, Castleford, Idaho

(PICTURED ON PAGE 53)

    2 cups milk
    4 cups (about 2 pounds) potatoes, peeled and sliced 1/4-in. thick
  1/4 teaspoon oregano
  1/4 teaspoon thyme
  1/4 teaspoon rosemary
    2 cloves garlic, minced (optional)
  1/2 teaspoon salt OR to taste
  1/8 teaspoon white pepper
    1 cup Gouda cheese, shredded
About 1 cup light cream OR half-and-half

Heat milk in large saucepan; add potatoes and seasoning. Cook about 20 minutes, stirring often. Layer in greased baking dish with shredded cheese. Pour cream over all. Bake at 350° for 30 minutes or until potatoes are tender. **Yield:** 4-6 servings.

APPLE/CHEESE BARS
Vicki Raatz, Waterloo, Wisconsin

(PICTURED ON PAGE 54)

CRUST:
  1/2 cup granulated sugar
    1 cup butter, softened
    2 eggs, *separated*
    1 teaspoon baking powder
  1/2 teaspoon salt
    2 cups all-purpose flour (can use part rolled oats, if desired)

FILLING:
    4 medium size cooking apples (about 4 cups), grated
    1 package (8 ounces) finely grated cheddar cheese
  1/4 cup flour
  3/4 cup granulated sugar
    1 teaspoon ground cinnamon

TOPPING:
Reserved egg whites
  1/4 cup cream cheese, softened
1-1/2 cups confectioners' sugar

Make crust by combining sugar, butter, *egg yolks,* baking powder, salt and flour. Blend until mixture is crumbly. Press 1/2 of mixture into bottom of 13-x 9-in. baking pan; reserve remaining half. Set aside. Grate apples and cheese together in one bowl (food processor works well for this). Add sugar, flour and cinnamon; mix well. Spread apple/cheese filling over crust. Sprinkle re-

maining half of crumb mixture over filling. Make topping by whipping egg whites until peaks form. Gradually add confectioners' sugar and cream cheese, beating continuously. Spoon evenly over all layers. Bake at 350° for 30-35 minutes or until light golden brown. **Yield:** 36 bars.

HARVEST GRAPE PIE
Jeannette Mack, Rushville, New York

(PICTURED ON PAGE 54)

Pastry for two-crust pie

FILLING:
5-1/3 cups Concord grapes
1-1/3 cups granulated sugar
  1/4 cup flour
1-1/4 teaspoons fresh lemon juice
Dash salt
1-1/2 tablespoons butter

Remove and save skins from grapes by pinching grapes at end opposite stem (pulp pops out). Put pulp in saucepan without water; bring to rolling boil. While mixture is hot, rub through strainer (or use food mill) to remove seeds. Mix strained pulp with reserved grape skins. Combine sugar and flour; mix lightly through grape mixture. Sprinkle with lemon juice and salt. Pour grape mixture into pastry-lined pie pan. Dot with butter. Cover with top crust OR use decorative pastry cutouts for top crust. Cut slits in top crust; seal and flute edges. Bake at 425° for 35-45 minutes or until top crust is nicely browned and juice is thickened. Cool before serving.

FRESH CALIFORNIA SALSA
M. Jessie Gates, Riverside, California

(PICTURED ON PAGE 53)

    1 pint canned tomatoes, chopped
    2 medium size fresh tomatoes, diced
    1 can (4-ounces) green chilies
    1 bunch green onions, diced
  1/2 bunch fresh cilantro leaves, minced
    2 tablespoons cider vinegar
    1 teaspoon salt

Combine all ingredients; mix well. Refrigerate, covered, a minimum of one hour. Serve with tortilla chips.

PEACH PRALINE PIE
Elizabeth Hunter, Prosperity, South Carolina

(PICTURED ON PAGE 54)

- 4 cups (about 3 pounds) peeled, sliced ripe peaches
- 1/2 cup granulated sugar
- 2 tablespoons quick-cooking tapioca
- 1 teaspoon lemon juice

PRALINE LAYER:
- 1/2 cup all-purpose flour
- 1/4 cup brown sugar, firmly packed
- 1/2 cup chopped pecans
- 1/4 cup butter OR margarine
- 1 9-inch *unbaked* pie shell*

Combine peaches, sugar, tapioca and lemon juice in large bowl; let stand 15 minutes. Combine flour, brown sugar and pecans in small bowl; cut in butter with fork or mix with fingertips until mixture is crumbly. (Makes 1-1/3 cups.) Sprinkle 1/3 of praline mixture over bottom of pie shell; cover with peach mixture. Sprinkle remaining praline mixture over peaches, allowing peach layer to show, if desired. Bake at 450° for 10 minutes; reduce heat to 350° and bake for 20 minutes longer or until peaches are tender and topping is golden brown. *(Deep dish frozen pie shell works well for this pie.)

POUND CAKE
Paula Higgenbotham, Lilburn, Georgia

(PICTURED ON PAGE 54)

- 1 cup butter OR margarine, softened
- 3 cups granulated sugar
- 6 eggs, room temperature
- 3 cups all-purpose flour
- 1/4 teaspoon baking soda
- 3/4 teaspoon salt
- 1 cup sour cream, room temperature
- 1 teaspoon vanilla extract
- 1/2 to 1 teaspoon almond extract

- 2 cups *finely* chopped, peeled peaches
- Whipped cream

Cream butter and sugar together until light and fluffy. Add eggs one at a time, mixing after each. Combine flour, soda and salt in a separate bowl. Add dry ingredients alternately with sour cream to creamed ingredients. Stir in extracts. Bake at 350° in a greased and floured 10-in. tube or bundt pan for 70-80 minutes OR in two 9- x 5-in. loaf pans for 1 hour. Remove from pans to cooling rack. Dust with confectioners' sugar OR serve with fresh peaches and whipped cream if desired.

ONIONS AND STIR-FRY BEEF
Brenda Masters, Palmyra, Missouri

(PICTURED ON PAGE 56)

- 1 pound *lean* beef steak (flank, sirloin or top round) cut into 1/4-inch-thick strips
- 1 teaspoon salt
- 1 egg white
- 1 tablespoon cornstarch
- About 2 tablespoons vegetable oil, more as needed
- 3 cups mild onions, sliced
- 1 tablespoon dry wine or sherry OR wine vinegar
- 1 tablespoon sugar
- 4 tablespoons Lite soy sauce
- Broccoli cuts, carrot diagonals (optional)

Combine beef, salt, egg white and cornstarch. Mix well with hands; set aside. Heat oil to 375° in wok or deep skillet. Stir-fry beef (small amounts at a time) until lightly browned; drain on paper towels. Lower temperature to 350°; add additional oil if necessary and stir-fry onions until soft and well-browned. Remove. Add broccoli and carrots if desired; stir-fry until tender/crisp. Add beef and onions, wine/sherry/vinegar, sugar and soy sauce. Stir-fry 2 minutes at 425° until beef is glazed and brown. Serve on a bed of rice. **Yield:** 4 servings.

ONION BREAD KUCHEN APPETIZER
Margo Varo, Eastman, Wisconsin

(PICTURED ON PAGE 56)

- 1 loaf frozen bread dough, *thawed*
- 1 pound onions, diced
- 4 tablespoons butter
- 2 ounces thin-sliced ham, diced
- 2 eggs
- 1/2 cup sour cream
- Salt to taste
- Caraway seed

Roll bread dough out on greased cookie sheet, forming slight rim around edges, and set aside. Saute onions in butter in skillet until clear; mix in ham, eggs, sour cream and seasonings. Spread over dough. Bake at 350° for 15-20 minutes or until dough is golden brown on top. Remove from oven; cut into small squares. **Yield:** 30 appetizers. **Diabetic Exchanges:** One serving equals 1/2 bread, 1/2 vegetable, 1/2 fat; also, 72 calories, 117 mg sodium, 25 mg cholesterol, 8 gm carbohydrate, 3 gm protein, 3 gm fat.

ONION/BACON OATMEAL BUNS
Lila McNamara, Dickinson, North Dakota

(PICTURED ON PAGE 56)

- 2 cups boiling water
- 1 cup quick-cooking oats
- 3 tablespoons vegetable oil
- 2 packages quick-rise dry yeast
- 1/3 cup warm water (110°-115°)
- 1/4 cup dark molasses
- 2/3 cup brown sugar
- 1 egg
- 2 teaspoons salt
- About 6 cups all-purpose flour, more as needed
- 3/4 pound bacon, cut in 1/4-inch pieces, fried but not too crisp
- 2 cups diced onion, sauteed until slightly brown in bacon drippings

Pour boiling water over oats; cool. Add oil, yeast softened in 1/3 cup water, molasses, brown sugar, egg and salt. Beat in 1/2 flour to make soft dough; add bacon and onion pieces. Add remaining flour; knead until smooth. Cover bowl with foil; let dough rise until doubled in bulk. Punch down; let rise again. Pull off lemon-sized pieces; form into round bun shapes; place on greased baking sheets. Let rise until doubled in bulk. Bake at 375° for 18-20 minutes. Brush with melted butter while still hot. Cool. **Yield:** 30 buns. **Diabetic Exchanges:** One serving equals 2 bread, 1/2 fat; also, 170 calories, 186 mg sodium, 11 mg cholesterol, 29 gm carbohydrate, 5 gm protein, 4 gm fat.

ONION ODORS
- You can wash onion odors from your hands with fresh undiluted lemon juice or a weak ammonia rinse.
- Rub each finger *vigorously* with celery salt before washing, to rid hands of onion odors.
- Wash each hand with cold water and salt, then rub chlorophyll toothpaste over fingers and rinse well.

FRENCH ONION CASSEROLE
Shirley Wilson, Elmwood, Illinois

(PICTURED ON PAGE 57)

2 large, white sweet onions, peeled and sliced 1/4 inch thick
3 tablespoons butter
1/2 pound Swiss cheese, grated
1 can (10-3/4 ounces) cream of chicken soup
1/2 cup milk
1 teaspoon Lite soy sauce
8 slices French bread, 1/4 inch thick, *buttered*

Saute onion in butter until tender; spoon into 11- x 7-in. glass dish. Spread cheese over onions. Heat soup, milk and soy sauce together until well-blended; pour over onions and cheese. Mix gently with fork. Place buttered bread slices on top, overlapping if necessary. Bake, uncovered, at 350° for 30 minutes. **Yield:** 6-8 servings.

ONION LORE
● Dice more onions than you need, then freeze the leftovers in well-wrapped 1/2 cup portions in muffin tins. Store these handy ready-to-use portions in heavy plastic bags.
● Leftover onions keep much longer in the refrigerator if you use the top first and leave the root uncut.
● Put a toothpick in any whole garlic cloves you add to meats, stews and salad dressings—they'll slip out easily after cooking.
● Store garlic cloves refrigerated in a little olive oil, and they'll keep indefinitely.

RUSSIAN LEEK SOUP
Joyce Molzen, Lovington, Illinois

(PICTURED ON PAGE 57)

5 tablespoons butter
2 cups leeks, chopped
1 pound fresh mushrooms, sliced
1-1/2 cups carrots, thinly sliced
6 cups chicken broth OR 1 can (49-1/2 ounces)
2 teaspoons dill weed
1-2 teaspoons salt OR to taste
1/4 teaspoon pepper
1 bay leaf
5 cups potatoes, diced
1 cup half-and-half

Melt butter in large skillet; saute leeks, mushrooms and carrots for 5 minutes.

Stir in broth, dill weed, salt, pepper and bay leaf. Add potatoes; cook until tender, about 20 minutes. Add half-and-half; cook until thickened. **Yield:** 8-10 servings.

HAMMERLOCK ONIONS
Ann Bates, Rathdrum, Idaho

(PICTURED ON PAGE 57)

4 large Walla Walla sweet onions, sliced 1/4 inch thick

MARINADE:
1 cup apple cider vinegar
1 cup sugar

DRESSING:
1/3 cup mayonnaise
2/3 cup sour cream
1-1/2 teaspoons celery seed*
1/2 teaspoon salt*

*Can substitute 1 tablespoon celery salt instead of celery seed and salt. Place sliced onions in bowl; set aside. Bring vinegar and sugar to boil. Remove from stove; pour over onions. Mix well; refrigerate at least 8 hours or overnight. Drain and squeeze out excess moisture; combine with dressing ingredients and chill till serving time. **Yield:** 20 servings.

GREEN ONION OMELET
Georgia Ebright, Lyons, Kansas

(PICTURED ON PAGE 57)

6 slices bacon, crisply fried and crumbled
2 bunches green onions, tops and all, chopped in 1/4-inch pieces
8 eggs
1/2 cup milk
1 teaspoon salt OR to taste
1/4 to 1/2 teaspoon pepper

Using crumbled bacon and about 1 tablespoon bacon drippings, cook onions over low heat until wilted, stirring frequently. Mix eggs, milk, salt and pepper with fork until blended; pour eggs, all at once, into skillet over bacon/onions. Stir with fork to spread eggs over bottom of skillet. Reduce heat. Lift edges of omelet with spatula allowing uncooked eggs to cook around edges. Cook until eggs are puffy and set; serve immediately. **Yield:** 4-6 servings.

CHICKEN WITH 40 CLOVES OF GARLIC
Mary Swetich, Ely, Nevada

(PICTURED ON PAGE 57)

40 small cloves garlic, *unpeeled* (about 2 or 3 bulbs)
1 fryer chicken, cut into pieces
1/2 cup dry white wine OR wine vinegar
1/4 cup olive oil
1 teaspoon dried thyme leaves
1/2 teaspoon dried sage leaves
1 tablespoon fresh minced parsley
4 small bay leaves
1 teaspoon salt OR to taste
1/4 teaspoon pepper
French bread

Scatter garlic cloves over bottom of Dutch oven. Place chicken pieces over garlic, skin side up. Sprinkle wine/vinegar, oil and seasonings over chicken; cover pan tightly with foil *and* lid. *NO STEAM SHOULD ESCAPE DURING BAKING.* Bake at 375° for 1 hour (remove lid during last 10 minutes of baking to brown slightly, if desired). Discard bay leaves; place chicken on platter. Squeeze garlic from skins onto French bread—it will taste surprisingly mild! **Yield:** 4-5 servings.

BAKED ONIONS WITH DILL
Erna Sobkow, Calder, Saskatchewan

(PICTURED ON PAGE 58)

6 medium onions
6 slices bacon
1/4 cup tomato juice
2 tablespoons bacon drippings
2 tablespoons brown sugar
1 teaspoon salt
1/4 teaspoon pepper
1/4 teaspoon paprika
1/2 teaspoon dill *seeds*
Chopped fresh parsley

Peel onions; cut crosswise into halves. Place cut sides up in greased 10- x 6- x 2-in. baking pan. Fry bacon until crisp; drain and crumble over onions. Combine tomato juice, bacon drippings, brown sugar, salt, pepper, paprika and dill seeds; pour over onions. Cover with foil; bake at 325° about 1 hour or until tender, basting occasionally. Sprinkle with parsley at serving time. (Serving suggestion: This dish is great with roast beef!) **Yield:** 6 servings. **Diabetic Exchanges:** One serving equals 2 vegetable, 2 fat; also, 134 calories, 469 mg sodium, 5 mg cholesterol, 12 gm carbohydrate, 3 gm protein, 9 gm fat.

ONION-ITALIAN SAUSAGE
Ruth Van Der Leest, Lyndon, Illinois

(PICTURED ON PAGE 58)

- 2 tablespoons butter
- 6 medium onions, peeled and sliced 1/4 inch thick
- 6 sweet Italian sausages
- 1 small green pepper, chopped
- 1 small red pepper, chopped
- 1-1/2 tablespoons salt-free Italian seasonings

Dash Lite soy sauce

Melt butter in large skillet; add onions and cook until lightly browned. Remove; set aside. Brown sausages lightly in skillet, turning frequently. Remove; set aside with onions. Add more butter to skillet if necessary and lightly brown peppers. Add onions, sausages, Italian seasonings and soy sauce to skillet. Add water to 1-in. depth and simmer until sausages are done and water is cooked away. Serve with buns. **Yield:** 6 servings. **Diabetic Exchanges:** One serving equals 2 protein, 2 vegetable, 2 fat; also, 287 calories, 674 mg sodium, 64 mg cholesterol, 9 gm carbohydrate, 15 gm protein, 21 gm fat.

CREAM OF LEEK SOUP
Yvonne Crimbring, Canton, Pennsylvania

(PICTURED ON PAGE 58)

- 1 pound leeks*
- 1 cup butter
- 1 cup flour
- 1 quart chicken stock OR 4 bouillon cubes dissolved in 1 quart hot water
- 1 quart half-and-half
- 1/2 teaspoon salt OR to taste
- 1/4 teaspoon pepper
- 1 cup cooked potato, diced
- 1 cup ham, diced

*Can substitute combination of green onions and sweet white onions. Clean leeks carefully, rinsing well to remove soil. Cut into 1/2-in. pieces. Steam in covered container with 1/2 cup water until tender (can do this in microwave); *DO NOT DRAIN.* Set aside. Melt butter in saucepan; add flour, stirring constantly until smooth. Cook 2 to 4 minutes over low heat, stirring constantly until flour is thoroughly cooked. Grad-

ually add chicken stock, stirring with wire whisk; bring to boil. Turn heat to low; add half-and-half, seasonings, leeks, potato and ham. *DO NOT BOIL.* **Yield:** About 4 quarts.

GARLIC ROASTED POTATOES
Margaret Somerville, Elk Creek, California

(PICTURED ON PAGE 58)

- 4 large baking potatoes, peeled
- 4 cloves garlic
- 6 tablespoons butter
- 3/4 cup grated Parmesan cheese, *divided*

Salt to taste
Pepper to taste

Cut potatoes in half lengthwise; slice 1/4 in. thick. Rinse in cold water; drain thoroughly on paper towels. Mince garlic or put through press. Melt butter in small saucepan; add garlic and cook on medium heat for 1 minute. Place potatoes in large bowl; add butter/garlic, *half the cheese* and seasonings. Stir until potatoes are well-coated; pour into greased shallow dish. Top with remaining cheese; bake at 400°, uncovered, until golden brown, about 30 minutes. *Do not stir or turn during baking.* **Yield:** 8 servings. **Diabetic Exchanges:** One serving equals 1/2 protein, 1 bread, 1-1/2 fat; also, 192 calories, 190 mg sodium, 32 mg cholesterol, 17 mg carbohydrate, 6 gm protein, 12 gm fat.

GARLIC GUIDES

● Saute garlic gently—do not brown —to avoid bitter flavor.

● For great taste, make small slits in pork or lamb and insert whole cloves of garlic just before roasting.

CHEESE PUFFS
Margaret Uhen, Waukesha, Wisconsin

- 3 green onions, finely chopped
- 1 cup grated cheddar cheese
- 1/2 cup mayonnaise
- 24 toast rounds

Combine onions with cheese and mayonnaise. Spread on toast rounds. In shallow baking dish, microwave half the rounds for 1-1/2 to 2-1/2 minutes (or until bubbly) at 50-60% power. Turn baking dish once during cooking. Repeat with remaining puffs. Serve hot. **Yield:** 24 appetizers.

BARBECUED SHRIMP KABOBS WITH VEGETABLE POCKETS
Mary Boyd, Mountainair, New Mexico

KABOBS:
- 8 strips bacon, cut into quarters
- 16 cherry tomatoes OR Roma tomato chunks
- 32 medium fresh shrimp, shelled and cleaned (about 2 pounds)
- 2 cans (8-ounce each) button mushrooms, drained (reserve liquid)
- 8 metal skewers

POCKETS:
- 8 sheets heavy-duty foil
- 1 red bell pepper, sliced in thin strips
- 1 green bell pepper, sliced in thin strips
- 1 medium zucchini, peeled and cubed
- 1/2 cup green onions, chopped
- 2 teaspoons salt
- 1 teaspoon pepper
- 4 teaspoons sesame seeds
- 4 teaspoons fresh parsley, chopped
- 8 tablespoons butter

BASTING SAUCE:
- 1/4 cup vegetable oil
- 2 tablespoons reduced-sodium soy sauce
- 1 tablespoon lemon juice
- 1/2 teaspoon pepper
- 1/2 teaspoon thyme
- 1/2 teaspoon basil
- 1/2 teaspoon marjoram

Shell shrimp by inserting fork under shell, lifting and peeling shell away. Clean shrimp by removing vein (dark line) with clean paper towel. Skewer each shrimp twice. Form kabobs by alternating bacon, tomatoes, shrimp and mushrooms on skewers. Refrigerate while preparing vegetable pockets. Make these by folding each sheet of foil in half. Crimp sides tightly, leaving top of pocket open. Divide vegetables into eight equal portions; place in pockets and add divided portions of salt, pepper, sesame seeds and parsley. Dot with butter; add 2 tablespoons of reserved mushroom liquid to each. Fold tops over; crimp tightly. Place pockets on medium-heat coals; cook for 10-15 minutes. After 3-5 minutes, put kabobs on grill; turn often and baste with sauce. (Shrimp cooks quickly, 7-10 minutes.) Serve 1 kabob and 1 pocket per person. **Yield:** 8 servings.

LEMON GARLIC BAKED CHICKEN
Bobbie Zylstra, Everson, Washington

- 1 2- to 2-1/2-pound frying chicken, cut up
- 1 large clove garlic, crushed
- 1/2 teaspoon salt
- 2 teaspoons rosemary
- Several grinds fresh black pepper
- 1 teaspoon grated lemon rind
- 1/3 cup lemon juice
- 1/3 cup water

Rinse chicken; pat dry. Place, skin side down, in 13- x 9- x 2-in. baking pan. Combine garlic, salt, rosemary, pepper and lemon rind. Sprinkle mixture over chicken. Pour lemon juice and water over all. Bake, uncovered, at 400° for 30 minutes. Turn chicken pieces. Baste with pan liquids. Bake for 30 minutes more or until tender. **Yield:** 4 servings. **Diabetic Exchanges:** One serving equals the following—4 protein, 1-1/2 fat. One serving yields: 333 mg sodium, 109 mg cholesterol.

LAYERED MEXICAN DIP
Margaret Bailey, Coffeeville, Mississippi

- 2 cans (16 ounces *each*) refried beans
- 2 avocados, mashed
- 1 tablespoon lemon juice
- 1 carton (16 ounces) cultured sour cream
- 1 package taco seasoning mix
- 8 ounces grated cheddar cheese
- 1/2 teaspoon chili powder
- 2 bunches green onions, chopped coarsely
- 1 can (16 ounces) black olives
- Corn chips

Spread beans on bottom of 10-in. square serving dish or platter. Mash avocados with lemon juice; layer on top of beans. Combine sour cream and taco seasoning mix; spread on top of avocado layer. Toss cheese and chili powder together; layer on top of sour cream. Top with onions and black olives. Serve with corn chips.

CHICKEN KIEV (MICROWAVE)
Janice Thompson, Martin, Michigan

- 2/3 cup melted butter
- 3/4 cup dry bread crumbs OR crushed corn flakes
- 3 tablespoons grated Parmesan cheese
- 1 teaspoon basil
- 1 teaspoon oregano
- 1/2 teaspoon garlic salt
- 1/4 teaspoon salt
- 2 chicken breasts, split, boned and skinned

SAUCE:
- 1/2 cup apple juice OR white wine
- 1/2 cup chopped green onion
- 1/4 cup chopped fresh parsley
- Reserved butter

Melt butter in glass mixing bowl in microwave for 40 seconds on HIGH. Dip chicken breasts in melted butter. Combine crumbs, cheese, spices and salts. Dip chicken in crumb mixture to coat. Set aside unused melted butter. Arrange chicken in 13- x 9- x 2-in. glass baking dish. Microwave on HIGH for 9 minutes. Rotate dish a half turn; cook approximately 9 minutes longer (or until fork tender). Combine sauce ingredients, including reserved butter, and pour over chicken. Cover with waxed paper and microwave 3 to 5 minutes on 70% POWER or 1-1/2 to 2 minutes on HIGH. Let stand, covered, for 5-6 minutes. Spoon sauce over chicken and serve hot. **Yield:** 4-6 servings.

BOMBAY CHICKEN SALAD
Billie Mahaney, Santa Cruz, California

- 1 cup bulgur
- 2 cups water
- 1 teaspoon salt
- 1 teaspoon curry powder
- 1 package (10-ounce) frozen peas, parcooked, drained
- 1/4 cup salted peanuts
- 2 cups diced, cooked chicken
- 2 tablespoons sliced green onions

DRESSING:
- 1/2 cup mayonnaise
- 1/2 cup plain yogurt
- 2 tablespoons orange marmalade
- 1 teaspoon Dijon mustard
- 1 teaspoon salt

Boil 2 cups water; add bulgur and salt. Cover; let stand 1 hour. Meanwhile, combine curry powder, peas, peanuts, chicken and onion in large bowl. Set aside. Combine dressing ingredients; chill. Add prepared bulgur to salad mixture; add dressing and mix gently. For best flavor, let salad chill overnight. Garnish salad with additional peanuts and orange slices, if desired. **Yield:** 6-8 servings.

CHICKEN PARMESAN
Vonda Miller, Osgood, Indiana

- 1/4 cup butter
- 1/2 cup Parmesan cheese
- 1/2 cup bread crumbs
- 1 tablespoon paprika
- 1/4 to 1/2 teaspoon garlic powder
- 1-1/2 teaspoons Italian seasoning OR 1/2 teaspoon each of rosemary, oregano, basil
- 6 chicken breast *halves**, boned, skinned (1-1/2 pounds)

*Chicken parts may be substituted for chicken breasts—allow *7 minutes per pound of chicken* for cooking. Melt butter in 8- x 12-in. glass pan. Dip both sides of chicken in butter. Combine remaining ingredients on paper plate; roll chicken in mixture. Place chicken in dish, with thicker edges toward outside. Cover loosely with waxed paper. Microwave on HIGH for 12 minutes, rotating dish once. **Yield:** 6 servings. **Conventional Method:** Omit waxed paper. Bake at 350° for 35-45 minutes. **Diabetic Exchanges:** One serving equals 3 protein, 1/2 bread, 1 fat; also, 283 calories, 284 mg sodium, 114 mg cholesterol, 7 gm carbohydrate.

TERIYAKI CHICKEN
Meg Jordan, Riley, Oregon

MARINADE:
- 1/2 cup vegetable oil
- 1 cup reduced-sodium soy sauce
- 3 tablespoons brown sugar
- 3 garlic cloves, mashed
- 1 tablespoon grated fresh ginger root OR 1/8 teaspoon powdered ginger
- 2 tablespoons sherry OR white wine OR apple juice
- 1 fryer chicken (3- to 3-1/2-pound), *skin removed,* cut in pieces

Combine all marinade ingredients in jar. Cover; shake well. Place chicken in large zip-lock plastic bag; pour in marinade. Seal; refrigerate from 2-24 hours. Turn once. Drain excess moisture from chicken. Cook over medium coals for 40-45 minutes, turning several times and brushing with marinade. (Or, parcook in microwave, covered with plastic wrap, for 15 minutes.) Finish on grill only until pieces are cooked but not dry (about 10 minutes). Good hot or cold. **Yield:** 4 servings.

BARBECUE EXTRAS

● **Savory Spuds.** For "better-than-baked" potatoes, make 1/4-in. cuts and spread potato surfaces with a mixture of 1 tablespoon butter, 1 tablespoon Parmesan cheese and 1 tablespoon bacon bits. Sprinkle with garlic powder. Wrap and grill as usual.

● **Onion Spuds.** Precook 4 unpared potatoes in the oven or microwave until partially baked; cool. Slice 3/4 of the way through potato (every 1/8 in.) Mix 1/2 package dry onion soup mix with 4 tablespoons melted butter; drizzle between slices and over potatoes. Wrap and grill.

BEEF AND BACON TWIRLS
Patricia Rutherford, Winchester, Illinois

    1-1/2 pounds round steak,
           trimmed of fat
    Meat tenderizer
       1/2 pound sliced bacon
       1/4 to 1/2 teaspoon garlic
           powder
    Salt to taste
    Fresh-ground pepper
         2 tablespoons minced fresh
           parsley

Pound steak to 1/2-in. thickness or less. Use meat tenderizer according to package directions (may substitute thin mixture of catsup and mustard). Fry or microwave bacon until nearly done *but not crisp.* Sprinkle steak with garlic, pepper and parsley. Place bacon strips lengthwise on steak. Roll up jelly-roll style, starting with narrow end. Skewer with wooden picks at 1-in. intervals. Cut in 1-in. slices with serrated knife. Grill over hot coals, 8-10 minutes, turning once. Remove wooden picks. **Yield:** 6 servings. **Diabetic Exchanges:** One serving equals 4 protein; also, 277 calories, 183 mg sodium, 127 mg cholesterol, 1 gm carbohydrate.

BARBECUED LEG OF LAMB
Susan Nelson, Redwood Falls, Minnesota

    1 leg of lamb, butterflied
       (boneless)

MARINADE:
       1 to 2 large cloves garlic
     1/2 teaspoon salt
       2 tablespoons Dijon mustard
       1 tablespoon reduced-sodium
          soy sauce
       2 tablespoons lemon juice
    1-1/2 teaspoons ground rosemary
          OR thyme OR oregano
     1/4 cup olive oil OR
          vegetable oil

Debone leg of lamb; set aside. Prepare marinade by mashing garlic and salt with fork. Add mustard, soy sauce, lemon juice, herbs and oil; mix well. Brush each side of lamb with marinade. Place in large zip-lock plastic bag. Seal; refrigerate. For medium rare, grill on *greased* grill (4 in. from coals) 15-30 minutes per side (depends on thickness of cut). Baste frequently. Remove to serving platter; slice across grain. **Yield:** 14 servings. **Diabetic Exchanges:** One serving equals 5 protein, 2 fats; also 491 calories, 275 mg sodium, 243 mg cholesterol, 1 gm carbohydrate.

CHALUPAS
Virginia Crouse, Ashby, Nebraska

    2 fryer chickens (3 pounds
       each) OR 4 large chicken
       breasts, cooked, cubed
    1 pound grated cheddar
       cheese
   10 corn tortillas, cut in
       quarters
SAUCE:
    1 can (10-3/4 ounces) cream
       of mushroom soup
    1 can (10-3/4 ounces) cream
       of chicken soup
    1 cup sour cream
    1 can (4 ounces) diced green
       chilies
  2/3 cup milk
  1/2 cup finely diced onion
    1 jar (2 ounces) pimiento,
       chopped

Poach chicken or cook in microwave until tender; cool. Cut in cubes. Layer half of tortillas, chicken, sauce and cheese in buttered 13- x 9-in. baking dish. Repeat layers, ending with cheese. Bake, covered with foil, at 350° for 45

minutes; uncover and bake for 15 more minutes. (Dish can be made ahead and frozen.) **Yield:** 12-14 servings.

KOREAN BEEF BARBECUE (GALBI)
Linda Miller, Buffalo, North Dakota

MARINADE:
   10 green onions with stems,
       minced, OR 1/2 large white
       onion, chopped
    3 cloves garlic, minced
  1/4 cup reduced-sodium
       soy sauce
  1/2 teaspoon salt or to taste
       (optional)
    1 large teaspoon Accent or
       MSG (optional)
    3 heaping tablespoons toasted
       sesame seeds
  1/2 teaspoon pepper
    3 tablespoons sesame
       seed oil*
    3 tablespoons vegetable oil
    2 tablespoons to 1/4 cup
       honey
    2 tablespoons to 1/4 cup
       sugar

    1 sirloin tip roast (4-pound)
       OR thick-cut round steak
       OR sirloin steak, trimmed
       of fat

(*Sesame seed oil is available in health food stores or in larger grocery stores.) Mix marinade ingredients together in glass jar. Shake well. Cut meat in 1/8-in.-thick slices; pound to tenderize, if desired. Place meat and marinade in large zip-lock plastic bag. Seal; shake and turn to mix ingredients. Refrigerate overnight. Before grilling, drain excess moisture. Place a wire cooling rack over top of barbecue grill; lay meat strips on top of rack. (Or thread strips on bamboo skewers that have been soaked in water.) Grill over medium coals (meat cooks very quickly—5-8 minutes). Turn once. Serve hot or cold. **Yield:** 8-10 servings.

BARBECUE TIPS!

● Use only 1 layer of charcoal when grilling. This keeps the heat at 220°, ideal for most meats.

● Keep a loaded water pistol or squeeze bottle of water near the grill to prevent flaming (which burns meat).

● In a hurry? Before grilling, parcook some meats and poultry in the microwave oven or conventional oven or by simmering on top of stove. Parcooking (particularly in the microwave) saves time and keeps the meat's juiciness. This method is especially good for chicken halves.

65

The Seal Beach Inn and Gardens
212 5th St., Seal Beach, California 90740, 213/493-2416

Directions: From Los Angeles International Airport, take I-405 (San Diego Freeway) south to Seal Beach Blvd., south to Pacific Coast Highway, right to Fifth St., left 2 blocks to inn.

Schedule: Open year-round. Breakfast served daily 7:30-10:30 a.m. to inn guests; other meals and picnic baskets by special arrangement. Saturday and Sunday afternoon tea on occasion.

Accommodations: 23 rooms and suites with private baths, many with kitchenettes.

Rates: $78-$135 bed and breakfast for 2; corporate rates available upon request.

Visa, MasterCard, American Express accepted.

Hours and rates subject to change. Please call or write.

FROM THE morning buffet to occasional afternoon teas—which may include chicken salad sandwiches on zucchini bread, cinnamon-spiced whole hard-boiled eggs, heart-shaped scones with blackberry butter, lemon bread and chocolate-dipped shortbread hearts—the food here features California fruits and vegetables, and reflects a certain "fondness for chocolate".

CHOCOLATE ORANGE WREATH

One-half recipe Basic Rich Cream Yeast Dough (below)

BASIC RICH CREAM YEAST DOUGH
- 2 envelopes dry active yeast
- 1/2 cup warm water (110-115°)
- 1/2 pound butter, room temperature
- 6-1/2 cups flour
- 2-1/2 cups heavy cream
- 4 eggs
- 1/2 cup sugar
- 1 teaspoon salt

FILLING:
- 12 ounces cream cheese
- 1/3 cup sugar
- 2 tablespoons Grand Marnier *or* grated rind of 1 orange
- 1-1/2 cups coarsely grated semisweet chocolate

- 1/4 cup orange juice
- Coarse raw sugar
- Sliced almonds
- Orange zest
- Chocolate curls

Dissolve yeast in warm water; set aside. Slice butter into flour; cut in by hand or with mixer until mixture resembles coarse crumbs. In another bowl, combine yeast with remaining ingredients, mix well and add slowly to flour/butter mixture. Beat until thoroughly mixed. Place dough in plastic bag, allowing room for expansion. Store dough in refrigerator for up to 4 days. To make wreath, prepare dough first; then make filling. Combine cheese, sugar, Grand Marnier/orange peel. Roll dough to large rectangle. Spread cheese mixture on top of dough, top with grated chocolate. Starting at long edge of rectangle, roll dough. Form into circle on a parchment-lined

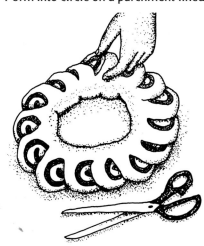

pan. Slice to create wreath shape. Brush with orange juice, top with coarse sugar, almonds and orange zest. Bake at 350° for 45 minutes or until brown. When cool, place chocolate curls on top. **Yield:** 20 servings.

INN-MADE GRANOLA

- 8 cups regular (old-fashioned) rolled oats
- 1-1/2 cups wheat germ
- 1/2 cup coconut
- 1 cup chopped dried fruit
- 1 cup sliced almonds
- 1-1/2 cups brown sugar, firmly packed
- 1-1/2 cups unprocessed bran
- 1 cup raisins
- 1 cup dried bananas
- 1 cup sunflower seeds
- 3/4 cup vegetable oil
- 1-1/4 cups honey
- 3 teaspoons vanilla

Combine oats, wheat germ, coconut, fruit, almonds, brown sugar, bran, raisins, bananas and seeds in large mixing bowl. Set aside. Heat oil, honey and vanilla and combine thoroughly with first mixture. Place on large cookie sheet. Bake at 350° for 30-40 minutes, stirring at 10 minute intervals until nicely browned. Stir granola as it cools to break up mixture. **Yield:** 16 servings.

COUNTRY plenty and a willingness to pass on a legacy of country cooking make Audrey Benson of Flagler, Colorado the "Best Cook in the Country", according to her daughter, Linda Bamber of Elkland, Missouri.

"The food on our table was always plentiful and delicious—the bounty of Mom's efforts. Homegrown chicken, fresh eggs, butter, fresh fruits and vegetables, row upon row of preserved produce and a full freezer kept us so well-fed we never knew how poor we were! It is a testimony to her cooking that we made it through those hard times loving ham, beans and cornbread!

"There are many good country cooks, but not all of them pass their legacy on. Mom passed her skills on to *all* her children. Needless to say, my sister and I were well tutored— and my *brothers* were accomplished cooks as well by the time they graduated from high school. They're adept at making light, fluffy pancakes, biscuits, yeast breads and a variety of sweets, in addition to main dishes, stews and casseroles.

"Although her days of cooking for harvest crews from Oklahoma to Canada are long gone, she may still be called upon to feed a crew and drive a truck all day, too. A delicious beef stew is left to simmer in the crockpot and the freezer yields date pinwheels and snickerdoodles. Piping hot cornbread rounds out an almost effortless meal. She's a prepared country cook!"

Audrey calls herself "a person who always has six people to cook for". She has created some recipes herself ... gotten some from other people ...adapted and changed some to suit her likes better. And, luckily for her family and friends, she's passed on her skills, as well as some of her favorite recipes!

SALT STICKS

2 cups lukewarm water (110-115°)
2 packages active dry yeast (2 tablespoons)
2 tablespoons sugar

5 to 5-1/2 cups flour
3/4 cup vegetable oil
1 beaten egg white
Seasoned salt, onion powder, coarse salt *or* cinnamon/sugar

Dissolve yeast in lukewarm water in large bowl. Stir in sugar, flour and oil. Knead on lightly floured board, about 5 minutes. Shape into a ball. Place in lightly greased bowl. Cover; let stand for 30 minutes. Divide into thirds. Pat out dough to cover 3 well-greased cookie sheets. Cut dough into sticks, 1-inch wide, 5 inches long, brush with beaten egg white. Top with desired seasoning. Bake at 400° for 18-20 minutes. Remove to cooling rack. **Yield:** 7-1/2 dozen sticks.

BAKED BEANS

1 quart cooked brown beans (could use Great Northerns), drained, rinsed
3/4 cup catsup
2 tablespoons prepared mustard
1 small chopped onion
2 tablespoons chopped green chilies
1/4 cup light molasses

Combine all ingredients in bean pot or 1-3/4 qt. casserole. Bake at 350°, covered, for 1 hour. (Can prepare in microwave on HIGH for 20 minutes.) **Yield:** 4-6 servings.

RICH CHOCOLATE CAKE

1 cup vegetable oil
1/2 cup cocoa
2 cups sugar
2 eggs
1/2 teaspoon salt
1 cup buttermilk
2-1/4 cups all-purpose flour
1 teaspoon vanilla
1 cup hot water
2 teaspoons baking soda

Combine oil, cocoa and sugar in mixing bowl and beat on low speed until well-mixed. Add eggs; beat on medium speed until well blended. Add salt, buttermilk, flour and vanilla. Add to mixture on low speed until combined; then beat on high speed for 2 minutes. Add soda to hot water; dissolve well. Add gradually to cake batter and mix just until combined. (Batter will be very thin before baking.) Bake in greased and floured 13-in x 9-in. x 2-in. baking pan (or 2 layer pans) at 375° for 40 minutes. Test with toothpick in center of cake for doneness. Frost with Chocolate Fudge Frosting, if desired.

CHOCOLATE FUDGE FROSTING

1 cup granulated sugar
4 tablespoons unsweetened cocoa
3/4 cup milk (whole milk is best)
1 tablespoon butter *or* margarine
1 teaspoon vanilla

Combine sugar, cocoa and milk in small heavy saucepan; cook until mixture begins to boil. Cover, cook for 2-3 minutes until steam washes sugar crystals down from sides of pan. Uncover, reduce heat and cook without stirring until mixture reaches soft ball stage (234°). Remove from heat. Cool mixture until it reaches temperature of 110°. Add butter and vanilla, stirring until butter is dissolved. Pour over warm cake. **Yield:** enough to cover a 13-in. x 9-in. x 2-in. cake. *Frosting not suitable for layer cake.*

FARM MARKET FRESH! Bushels of brightly polished red and green apples...brilliantly colored mounds of late summer and winter squash...gunny sacks bursting with freshly harvested potatoes —all sure signs of autumn along country roads.

Here's to the roadside entrepreneur who peddles produce with pride! Pack home a peck of harvest's best and celebrate the season with a lovely Pumpkin Soup ...creamy Cajun Cabbage...colorful Cranberry Orange Bread...rich Sweet Potato Pie or Souffle... savory "Feast" Pork Chops...or zesty Potato Romanoff, an easy-to-make cousin of popular twice-baked potatoes.

Try these recipes for a taste of autumn's bounty!

AUTUMN'S ABUNDANCE: Clockwise from lower left—Baked Cajun Cabbage (Pg. 75); Potato Romanoff (Pg. 75); Sweet Potato Souffle (Pg. 75); Pumpkin Soup (Pg. 76); Cranberry Orange Bread (Pg. 76); Sweet Potato Pie (Pg. 75); Squash Dressing (Pg. 75); "Feast" Pork Chops (Pg. 75).

AAH-H-H, APPLES! Is there anything that says "autumn" quite as well as apples?

Choose from popular red and golden Delicious apples...or old favorites such as Wealthy, Jonathan and Northern Spy. There are apples for every purpose, be it cooking, munching, pie baking or jelly making.

Gather up an orchard's finest and use them in our bound-to-please Taffy Apple Salad...Creamy Apple Tart...quick-and-easy Apple Squares...or old-fashioned rolled apple Dumplings.

Fill *your* kitchen with the luscious aroma of cooked apples.

APPETIZING APPLES! Clockwise from lower left—Quick Apple Dumplings (Pg. 76); Apple Cream Tart (Pg. 76); Taffy Apple Salad (Pg. 76); Creamy Apple Squares (Pg. 77).

Meals in Minutes

Recipes from Julianne Johnson, Grove City, Minnesota.

BUSY SCHEDULES demand meals that are on the table in a hurry—and this simple, satisfying menu fits the bill!

First, cook the rice, either on the stove top or in the microwave. Next, brown the turkey tenderloins or slices and then add the simple sauce ingredients for final simmering.

As the sauce simmers, put together the vegetable salad. It's made from ingredients that are usually on hand—add Parmesan cheese and croutons for variety.

And, what could be easier or quicker than the fruit dessert? Put it together while your family clears the dinner dishes!

It's delicious...and ready in less than half an hour!

TURKEY BREAST SUPREME

    1 tablespoon butter
1-1/2 pounds turkey breast slices
       OR 2 to 4 turkey breast
       tenderloins
  1/4 cup chopped green onion
    1 can (10-3/4 ounces) cream
       of chicken soup
  1/4 cup water
Freshly ground pepper
    1 cup (4 ounces) Swiss
       cheese, shredded

Melt butter in skillet on medium-high heat. Add turkey; brown on both sides. Add onion; saute 1-2 minutes. Stir in soup diluted with water; season with pepper. Reduce heat; cover and simmer 20 minutes. If using tenderloins, turn after 10 minutes. Remove turkey to heated serving dish. Add cheese to sauce remaining in skillet. Stir until melted. Pour cheese sauce over turkey. Serve turkey with cooked white rice or long grain/wild rice mix. Garnish with additional green onion, if desired.

MICROWAVE TIP: Wonder what kind of wrap to work with? Use paper towel when you want to absorb moisture, plastic wrap for steaming and waxed paper to prevent splatters.

MICROWAVE RICE

  1 cup long-grain rice
  2 cups water
  1 teaspoon salt
  1 tablespoon vegetable oil

Place all ingredients in a 3-qt. covered casserole. MW on HIGH for 8 minutes; stir. Let stand in microwave for 10 minutes; MW on HIGH for 5 minutes more. Let stand for 5 minutes. **Yield:** 4 servings.

WINTER VEGETABLE SALAD

   1 head iceberg lettuce,
      washed and chilled
   2 to 3 carrots, peeled—sliced
      or chopped
  12 to 16 stuffed green olives,
Purchased salad dressing of choice
Parmesan cheese (optional)
Croutons (optional)

Cut lettuce into narrow strips or tear and place on individual salad plates.

Add equally divided amounts of carrots and olives to each serving; top with dressing. (A creamy buttermilk salad dressing is especially good on this salad.)

CHERRY/NUT BANANA DESSERT

   4 ripe bananas, peeled
Whipped cream (in spray can)
  12 walnut halves, chopped
Maraschino cherries

Dice bananas and place in dessert dishes. Immediately before serving, top with whipped cream, nuts and cherries.

SALAD HINTS
● When buying iceberg lettuce, look for a head that's springy instead of solid when you squeeze it.
● Wash all salad greens and vegetables before use. Rinse greens first in lukewarm water to remove dirt; rinse again in cold water. Use salad spinner to remove excess moisture.

Wrap in paper towels; enclose in plastic bag and refrigerate.

GUESSING at what gifts to give? Look no further! Nothing can compare with home-baked gifts from a country kitchen!

These palate-pleasing recipes tempt every set of taste buds—from rich, fruit-and-nut dark breads to light, airy cream scones. Package handsome, fiber-rich Bran or Apple Pecan Coffee Cake in a reclaimed holiday tin. Bake miniature fruit and nut breads and wrap for school bus driver, mail carrier or next-door neighbor.

Also pictured here are several

spreads to go along with the breads. Fill pretty jars (labeled for *refrigerator storage*) with the spreads...then tie with a bright, holiday ribbon.

Whatever bread you bake or spread you make—for family or gift-giving—you'll be delivering a heaping helping of holiday cheer from your kitchen!

GREAT GIFTS. Clockwise from lower left—Crunchy Bran Coffee Cake (Pg. 78); Lemon Bread (Pg. 77); Apricot Bread/Spread (Pg. 77); Strawberry Nut Bread/Spread (Pg. 79); Apple Pecan Coffee Cake (Pg. 78); Poppyseed Bread (Pg. 78); Dark Fruit Bread (Pg. 78); Cream Scones/Lemon Curd (Pg. 77).

FLAVORFUL, FAST quick breads! They're a savory side dish, guaranteed to satisfy that craving for something warm and home-baked on a cold winter's night. And most of them can be stirred up and table-ready in an hour or less!

Bake up Pumpkin Ribbon Bread, with its cream cheese layer...Almond Tea Bread, with the rich flavors of almond paste and fruit...Butter Dips, savory with butter and cheese...or Apple Streusel Muffins or Bread, with their irresistible combination of apples and spice.

WRAP UP quick breads! Clockwise from top—Butter Dips (Pg. 79); Pumpkin Ribbon Bread (Pg. 79); Apple Streusel Muffins/Bread (Pg. 79); Almond Tea Bread (Pg. 79).

BAKED CAJUN CABBAGE
Rowena Champagne, New Iberia, Louisiana

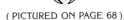

(PICTURED ON PAGE 68)

1 large head cabbage
1 cup chopped onions
1 cup chopped celery
1 cup chopped bell pepper

CHEESE SAUCE:
1/2 cup butter
4 tablespoons flour
1-1/2 cups milk
Salt
Cayenne pepper to taste
1/2 pound cheddar cheese, shredded

TOPPING:
1 cup chopped green onions
1/4 cup seasoned Italian bread crumbs

Remove outer leaves from cabbage. Cut into bite-size sections, removing heart. Boil about 10 minutes, uncovered, until tender/crisp. Drain; set aside. In separate saucepan, combine butter and flour, blending well over medium heat. Add onions, celery, pepper, salt and cayenne pepper. Saute for 10 minutes. Add milk, blending well over low heat until creamy. Add cheese; stir until smooth. Place cabbage in 2-quart casserole; top with seasoned cheese sauce. Sprinkle with green onions and bread crumbs. Bake at 350° for about 30 minutes. **Yield:** 6 servings.

SWEET POTATO SOUFFLE
Margaret Allen, Abingdon, Virginia

(PICTURED ON PAGE 68)

3 cups cooked, mashed sweet potatoes
3 eggs, *separated*
1/2 to 1 cup sugar
1 teaspoon vanilla
1/4 teaspoon nutmeg
1/4 to 1/2 cup melted butter
2 cups milk

TOPPING:
1/2 cup brown sugar
3 tablespoons melted butter
1/3 cup chopped nuts OR coconut

Bake pricked sweet potatoes at 400° until tender. Cool; peel and mash. Combine sweet potatoes with beaten egg *yolks* (reserve whites), sugar, vanilla, nutmeg, butter and milk. Set

aside. Beat the egg whites until stiff; carefully fold into sweet potato mixture. Pour into 2 quart greased baking dish. Combine topping ingredients; sprinkle over top in decorative pattern. Bake at 350° for 30 minutes. **Yield:** 10-12 servings.

POTATOES ROMANOFF
Jean Giesbrecht, American Falls, Idaho

(PICTURED ON PAGE 68)

6 medium baking potatoes
2 cups dairy sour cream
1 bunch green onions, chopped, about 1 cup
1-1/2 cups grated cheddar cheese
1-1/2 teaspoons salt
1/2 teaspoon pepper
Paprika

Cook unpeeled potatoes until tender, about 20-25 minutes. Cool; peel. Grate into large bowl; add remaining ingredients, except paprika. Mix well. Spoon into 13- x 9-in. baking dish. *Refrigerate 3-4 hours, covered, or overnight.* Bake at 350° for 40-50 minutes. Sprinkle with paprika. **Yield:** 8-10 servings.

"FEAST" PORK CHOPS
Barb Langan, Orland Park, Illinois

(PICTURED ON PAGE 69)

6 loin pork chops, 3/4 to 1 inch thick
Seasoned salt to taste
Seasoned pepper to taste
Garlic powder to taste
1 tablespoon butter

SIZZLE SAUCE:
3/4 cup apple juice OR cider
1/4 cup cider vinegar
2 tablespoons brown sugar
1-1/2 teaspoons molasses
1/2 teaspoon ground cloves
1-1/2 teaspoons dry mustard
1-1/2 teaspoons ginger

Season chops lightly with salt, pepper and garlic powder. Brown chops in butter in skillet on both sides. Add sauce ingredients (which have been combined) to skillet. Simmer, covered, for 20 minutes. Remove cover; simmer until sauce thickens. *Do not let burn.* (Chops may be grilled outdoors over hickory fire as prepared for annual Feast of the Hunters' Moon in Lafayette, Indiana, and finished off in simmered sauce.)

SWEET POTATO PIE
Evelyn Hill, Crisfield, Maryland

(PICTURED ON PAGE 69)

3 large *baked* sweet potatoes, about 2 cups
1/4 cup butter, melted
3/4 cup sugar
1/2 teaspoon salt
1 teaspoon vanilla extract
1/2 teaspoon lemon extract
2 eggs, *separated*
1 cup half-and-half OR evaporated milk
1 9-inch *unbaked* pie shell (deep dish)

(Bake potatoes at 400° until tender. Cool; remove skins.) Mash or whip potatoes in large mixing bowl. Add butter, sugar, salt and extracts. Set aside. In small bowl, beat egg yolks slightly. Add to potato mixture with milk/cream. Set aside. Whip egg whites until soft peaks form. Fold gently into potato mixture. Pour into pie shell. Bake at 425° for 15 minutes; reduce temperature to 350°; bake 25-30 minutes more until center tests done.

SQUASH DRESSING
Nila Tower, Baird, Texas

(PICTURED ON PAGE 69)

2 to 3 cups yellow squash, cubed (crookneck variety)
1 small onion, diced
2 cups crumbled corn bread
2 tablespoons butter OR margarine, melted
1 can (10-3/4 ounces) cream of chicken soup, undiluted
1 teaspoon poultry seasoning (marjoram, thyme, sage)
Salt to taste
Pepper to taste

Cook squash and onion in enough water for simmering, about 1-1/2 cups, until tender. Drain, *reserving 1 cup liquid.* Mix all ingredients lightly; place in 2-quart buttered casserole. Bake at 350° for 30 minutes or until light golden brown. **Yield:** 6-8 servings.

CRANBERRY ORANGE BREAD
Elaine Kremenak, Grants Pass, Oregon

(PICTURED ON PAGE 69)

- 2 cups all-purpose flour, *unsifted*
- 1-1/2 teaspoons baking powder
- 1 teaspoon baking soda
- 1/2 teaspoon salt
- 1 cup white sugar
- 1 egg, beaten
- 1/2 cup orange juice
- Grated rind of 1 orange
- 2 tablespoons melted butter
- 2 tablespoons hot water
- 1 cup raw whole cranberries
- 1 cup coarsely chopped walnuts

Combine flour, baking powder, soda, salt and sugar in large mixing bowl; set aside. Mix beaten egg with orange juice, rind, butter and hot water. Fold flour mixture into egg mixture until blended. *Do not beat.* Gently fold in cranberries and walnuts. Spoon into greased 9- x 6-in. loaf pan or smaller pans of choice. Bake at 325° for 60 minutes; test in center with wooden pick. Cool on rack for 15 minutes before removing from pans.

PUMPKIN SOUP
Shirley Van Garde, Brookings, Oregon

(PICTURED ON PAGE 69)

- 1/4 cup chopped green pepper
- 2 tablespoons chopped onion
- 1 teaspoon parsley flakes or fresh minced parsley
- 1/8 teaspoon thyme leaves
- 1 bay leaf
- 2 tablespoons butter
- 1 can (9 ounces) canned tomatoes, diced
- 2 cups mashed cooked pumpkin (or squash)
- 2 cups water
- 2 chicken bouillon cubes
- 1 tablespoon flour
- 2 cups milk
- 1 teaspoon salt
- 1/8 teaspoon pepper

Saute pepper, onion, parsley, thyme, and bay leaf in butter until tender; do not brown. Add tomatoes, pumpkin/squash, water and bouillon; bring to boil. Reduce heat; simmer 30 minutes, stirring occasionally. In small bowl, combine flour and milk; blend well. Stir into soup mixture; add salt and pepper. Cook over medium heat, stirring frequently until mixture boils. **Yield:** 6-8 servings.

QUICK APPLE DUMPLINGS (Rolls)
Florence Rasmussen, Amboy, Illinois

(PICTURED ON PAGE 70)

SYRUP:
- 2 cups water
- 1-1/2 cups sugar

DOUGH:
- 3 tablespoons vegetable shortening
- 2 cups flour
- 4 teaspoons baking powder
- Pinch salt
- 1 egg
- 1/2 cup milk

FILLING:
- 2-3 cups finely chopped apple
- 1/4 cup sugar
- 1/2-1 teaspoon cinnamon
- 1/4 teaspoon nutmeg
- Butter

Combine sugar and water in small saucepan; bring to boil. Pour into bottom of 13- x 9-in. baking pan. Set aside. Combine shortening, flour, baking powder and salt with mixer (or use food processor). Combine egg and milk; add to creamed mixture. Roll dough out between sheets of wax paper to 1/4-in. thickness. Remove top paper. Spread with filling ingredients which have been combined. Roll up like cinnamon rolls or noodles. Remove bottom paper. Slice into 8-10 rolls with sharp knife. Carefully lay rolls on top of syrup. Dot rolls with butter. Bake at 375° for 20-30 minutes or until golden brown. Serve hot or cold with milk, whipped cream or ice cream. **Yield:** 8-10 servings.

TAFFY APPLE SALAD
Jill Boyce, Zion, Illinois

(PICTURED ON PAGE 70)

SALAD DRESSING:
- 1 tablespoon flour
- 1/2 cup sugar
- 1 egg
- 2 tablespoons apple cider vinegar
- 1 can (8 ounces) crushed pineapple, *drained, reserve juice*
- 4 cups (1 pound) red Delicious apples, *unpeeled*
- 1 cup salted shelled peanuts
- 1 carton (8 ounces) nondairy topping

Combine flour and sugar; mix well. Beat egg; add to flour/sugar. Add vinegar and *reserved pineapple juice.* Cook in small pan on low heat. Stir and cook until thick. Cool. Pour cooled dressing over apples, pineapple and peanuts. Mix in nondairy topping. May sprinkle additional peanuts over top for garnish. **Yield:** 10 servings.

APPLE CREAM TART
Gladys Moran, Shohola, Pennsylvania

(PICTURED ON PAGE 70)

CRUST:
- 1-1/2 cups flour
- 3 tablespoons sugar
- 1/4 teaspoon salt
- 6 tablespoons butter

FILLING:
- 3 peeled, sliced apples to fill 9-inch springform pan
- 1/2 to 3/4 cup sugar
- 1 teaspoon cinnamon
- 1/4 teaspoon nutmeg

TOPPING:
- 2 egg yolks, beaten
- 1 cup heavy cream

Combine flour, sugar, salt and cut in butter until mixture resembles cornmeal. Press into bottom and up sides of 9-in. springform pan. Fill crust with sliced apples. Combine sugar, cinnamon and nutmeg; sprinkle over apples. Bake at 400° for 15 minutes. Combine egg yolks and cream; pour over fruit. Return to oven. Bake for 30 minutes or until apples are fork-tender. Cool on rack. **Yield:** 10 servings.

CREAMY APPLE SQUARES
Janet Woodburn, Caldwell, Idaho

(PICTURED ON PAGE 70)

- 1 package (18-1/2 ounces) yellow *pudding* cake mix
- 1/2 cup soft butter
- 1/4 cup brown sugar
- 1/2 teaspoon cinnamon
- 3 large red Delicious apples, thinly sliced, unpeeled
- 1 cup sour cream
- 1 egg

Combine cake mix and butter; mix until crumbly. *Reserve 2/3 cup for topping; add brown sugar and cinnamon to this reserved topping.* Mix well; set aside. Press remaining cake/butter mixture into bottom of ungreased 13- x 9-in. pan. Arrange apple slices over base. Blend sour cream and egg; spread evenly over apples. Sprinkle reserved topping mixture over all. Bake at 350° for 25-30 minutes or until topping is golden brown and bubbly. Serve warm. Refrigerate leftovers. **Yield:** 12-15 squares.

CREAM SCONES
Dorothy Child, Malone, New York

(PICTURED ON PAGE 72)

SCONES:
- 2 cups flour
- 3 teaspoons baking powder
- 1/2 teaspoon salt
- 2 tablespoons sugar
- 6 tablespoons butter OR shortening
- 2 eggs
- 1/2 cup light cream
- 2 tablespoons sugar

LEMON CURD:
- 4 tablespoons unsalted butter
- 1/2 cup sugar
- 1/2 cup fresh lemon juice
- 4 egg yolks, slightly beaten
- 1 tablespoon grated lemon rind, optional

Make scones by combining flour, baking powder, salt and sugar in medium bowl. Cut in butter/shortening until mixture resembles coarse crumbs. Set aside. In small bowl, beat eggs with fork; add cream. *Reserve 2 teaspoons of mixture.* Stir remaining egg mixture into flour mixture until just blended. Turn out onto floured board; knead *lightly.* Shape into 14- x 7-in. rectangle. Brush with reserved egg/cream

mixture. Sprinkle with sugar. Cut into 16 triangular pieces. Place about 1 in. apart on lightly floured cookie sheet. Bake at 425° for 8-10 minutes. Meanwhile, make lemon curd by combining butter, sugar, lemon juice and egg yolks in heavy saucepan over low heat (may use double boiler). Stir mixture constantly until it thickens enough to coat back of spoon (soft custard consistency). DO NOT BOIL OR MIXTURE WILL CURDLE. Stir in lemon peel, if desired. Pour into jar, seal and *refrigerate.* Serve warm scones with lemon curd or jam. **Yield:** 16 scones. **Diabetic Exchanges:** One serving equals 1 bread, 1 fruit, 1-1/2 fat; also, 212 calories, 198 mg sodium, 121 mg cholesterol, 23 gm carbohydrate, 4 gm protein, 8 gm fat.

APRICOT BREAD
Bev Bosveld, Waupun, Wisconsin

(PICTURED ON PAGE 72)

- 1 cup dried apricots
- 3/4 cup hot water
- 2 tablespoons butter, softened
- 1 cup sugar
- 1 egg
- 2 cups flour
- 1 teaspoon baking powder
- 1/4 teaspoon baking soda
- 1 teaspoon salt
- 1/2 cup orange juice
- 1/2 cup pecans, chopped

APRICOT SPREAD:
- 1 package (3 ounces) cream cheese, softened
- 2 tablespoons apricots, chopped and softened

Cut apricots into pieces in small bowl; pour hot water over all. Let soften for 30 minutes. Drain; *reserve 1/4 cup apricot water.* Set aside apricot pieces. Combine butter, sugar and egg in mixing bowl; cream well. In another bowl, combine flour, baking powder, soda and salt. Add dry ingredients to creamed mixture, alternately with apricot water and orange juice. Stir in apricot pieces and pecans. Spoon into greased and floured 9- x 5-in. loaf pan. Bake at 350° for 55-65 minutes or until bread tests done with wooden pick. Make apricot spread by combining ingredients. Refrigerate until serving time. (This bread's flavor improves with age.) **Yield:** 18 slices bread. **Diabetic Exchanges:** One serving equals 1 bread, 1 fruit, 1 fat; also, 179 calories, 183 mg sodium, 23 mg cholesterol, 30 gm carbohydrate, 3 gm protein, 5 gm fat.

LEMON BREAD
Caryn Wiggins, Columbus, Indiana

(PICTURED ON PAGE 72)

BREAD:
- 1 cup butter
- 2 cups sugar
- 4 eggs
- 1/2 teaspoon salt
- 1/2 teaspoon baking soda
- 3 cups all-purpose flour
- 1 cup buttermilk
- Grated rind of 1 lemon OR 1 tablespoon lemon peel spice
- 1 cup finely chopped pecans

GLAZE:
- Juice from 2 lemons OR 1/4 cup lemon juice
- 1 cup confectioners' sugar

Cream together butter and sugar in bowl on high speed of mixer. Blend in eggs, one at a time, beating after each addition. In another bowl, combine salt, soda and flour; add to creamed mixture alternately with buttermilk. Add lemon rind and nuts, stirring in by hand. Grease and flour one 9- x 5-in. loaf pan or two 7- x 3-in. pans. Then line bottom with parchment paper or waxed paper. Spoon batter into pan(s) and bake at 300° for 1 hour and 20 minutes or until bread tests done with wooden pick. Let bread cool in pans for 10 minutes; remove from pans to cooling racks. Combine glaze ingredients; punch holes in bread with toothpick while still warm. Pour glaze slowly over bread. Cool completely before slicing.

QUICK BREAD TIPS

- Fill pans about two-thirds full to allow for expansion of batter and give breads pretty, rounded shapes.
- Add a small amount of the recipe flour to raisins, dates and other dried fruits so they don't cling together when added to batter.
- Baking breads at high altitudes? Reduce baking powder or soda in each recipe by one-fourth. *Do not decrease* baking soda to less than 1/2 teaspoon per cup of sour milk used.
- Most quick breads are best stored at least overnight before slicing and serving.
- Cut quick breads with a thin, sharp knife or electric knife to prevent crumbling.
- For crusty biscuits, roll dough thinner, cut smaller and place farther apart on cookie sheet. For flaky biscuits, roll dough thicker, cut larger and place close together on cookie sheet.

DARK FRUIT BREAD
Lonna Pugh, Grandville, Michigan

(PICTURED ON PAGE 72)

- 1 package (15 ounces) raisins
- 2-1/4 cups water
- 4 tablespoons butter
- 2 cups sugar
- 2 eggs
- 1 teaspoon vanilla
- 1 package (16 ounces) pitted dates, chopped
- 5-1/2 cups all-purpose flour
- 4 teaspoons baking soda
- 1 teaspoon salt
- 1 can (20 ounces) crushed pineapple, *including juice*
- 1 cup coarsely chopped walnuts
- 1 jar (6 ounces) maraschino cherries, halved

In saucepan (or microwave) boil raisins in water until plumped, about 15 minutes. Drain raisins and save. Reserve liquid (about 2/3 to 3/4 cup). Cool; set aside. In large mixing bowl, cream butter, sugar, eggs and vanilla until fluffy. Add reserved liquid from raisins. In another bowl, combine drained raisins, dates and *1 cup* flour; stir into creamed mixture. Mix remaining flour with baking soda and salt; stir into mixture. Fold in pineapple, nuts and cherries. Fill clean, well-greased tin cans (16- to 20-oz. size) about two-thirds full of batter or four 7-1/2- x 3-1/2- x 3-in. loaf pans. Bake at 350° for 1 hour. **Yield:** 8 to 9 cans or 4 loaves.

CRUNCHY BRAN COFFEE CAKE
Gay Snyder, Stow, Ohio

(PICTURED ON PAGE 72)

- 1-1/4 cups boiling water
- 1 cup 100% OR unprocessed bran
- 1/2 cup butter
- 1/2 cup granulated sugar
- 1/2 cup brown sugar
- 2 eggs
- 1 teaspoon vanilla
- 1 teaspoon baking soda
- 1 teaspoon cinnamon
- 1/4 teaspoon salt
- 1-1/4 cups all-purpose flour

TOPPING:
- 3 tablespoons butter, melted
- 1/4 cup 100% bran
- 1/4 cup brown sugar
- 1/2 cup broken walnuts OR rolled oats

Combine boiling water and bran in small bowl; let stand for 2-3 minutes. In another bowl, cream together butter and sugars until light and fluffy. Add eggs, one at a time, beating after each addition; add vanilla. In another bowl, combine soda, cinnamon, salt and flour; mix into creamed mixture until blended. Add bran mixture; stir to blend. Pour into greased 9-in. round cake pan OR 8-in. square pan. Bake at 350° for 30-40 minutes. Make topping by combining ingredients; set aside. Remove coffee cake from oven; sprinkle topping over all. Broil 2-3 minutes until bubbly. **Yield:** 10 servings.

APPLE PECAN COFFEE CAKE
Ethel Hodges, Emporia, Kansas

(PICTURED ON PAGE 73)

CAKE:
- 1/2 cup vegetable shortening
- 1/2 cup butter, softened
- 1-1/2 cups sugar
- 2 eggs
- 3 cups all-purpose flour
- 2 teaspoons baking powder
- 1 teaspoon baking soda
- 1/4 teaspoon salt
- 1-3/4 cups buttermilk
- 2 medium apples, pared and thinly sliced

TOPPING:
- 1/2 cup flour
- 1/2 cup sugar
- 1-1/2 teaspoons cinnamon
- 3 tablespoons butter
- 1/2 cup coarsely chopped pecans

Cream shortening and butter together in large bowl. Add sugar gradually, beating until light and fluffy. Add eggs, one at a time, beating well after each addition. In another bowl, combine flour, baking powder, soda and salt; add to creamed mixture alternately with buttermilk. Spoon *half* of batter into greased and floured 13- x 9-in. baking pan or QUARTER batter into two 9-in. round cake pans. Arrange apple slices over top; spread with remaining batter. Prepare topping by combining flour, sugar and cinnamon. Cut in butter; stir in pecans. Sprinkle evenly over batter. Bake at 350° for 45 minutes or until cake tests done with wooden pick. **Yield:** 16 to 20 servings.

POPPYSEED BREAD
Tammy Flynn, Broken Bow, Nebraska

(PICTURED ON PAGE 73)

- 2-1/4 cups sugar
- 1-1/8 cups vegetable oil
- 3 eggs
- 1-1/2 teaspoons vanilla
- 1-1/2 teaspoons almond extract
- 1-1/2 teaspoons butter flavor extract
- 2 tablespoons poppyseed
- 3 cups all-purpose flour
- 1-1/2 teaspoons salt
- 1-1/2 teaspoons baking powder
- 1-1/2 cups milk

GLAZE:
- 1/4 cup orange juice
- 1/2 teaspoon vanilla
- 1/2 teaspoon butter flavor extract
- 1/2 teaspoon almond extract
- 3/4 cup confectioners' sugar

Combine sugar and oil in large bowl; beat until blended. Add eggs, one at a time, beating after each addition. Add flavorings and poppyseed; mix well. Set aside. In another bowl, combine flour, salt and baking powder. Add to creamed mixture, alternately with milk, until well blended. Pour into six 4-1/2- x 2-1/2-in. loaf pans, filling one-half to two-thirds full, or in miniature pans of choice. Bake at 350° for 45 minutes. Remove from oven; let cool 5 minutes in pans. Combine glaze ingredients; pour over breads while still in pans. Let stand 5 minutes more; remove from pans to cooling rack. **Yield:** 6 small loaves or 10 miniature loaves.

STRAWBERRY NUT BREAD
Maxine Davidson, Waynoka, Oklahoma

(PICTURED ON PAGE 73)

- 1 cup butter
- 1-1/2 cups sugar
- 1 teaspoon vanilla
- 1/4 teaspoon lemon extract
- 4 eggs
- 3 cups all-purpose flour
- 1 teaspoon salt
- 1 teaspoon cream of tartar
- 1/2 teaspoon baking soda
- 1 cup strawberry jam (freezer jam works well)
- 1/2 cup cultured sour cream
- 1/2 cup broken walnuts

STRAWBERRY SPREAD:
- 1 package (3 ounces) cream cheese, softened
- 2 tablespoons strawberry jam

Cream butter, sugar, vanilla and lemon extract together in large bowl until light and fluffy. Add eggs, one at a time, beating well after each addition. In another bowl, sift together flour, salt, cream of tartar and baking soda; set aside. In small bowl, combine jam and sour cream. Add dry ingredients to creamed mixture, alternately with jam/sour cream. Beat until well combined. Stir in nuts. Divide batter among nine greased and floured 4-1/2- x 2-1/2-in. loaf pans. Bake at 350° for 50 minutes or until wooden pick tests clean. Cool in pans for 10 minutes; remove from pans to cooling rack. Make spread by combining ingredients and *refrigerating* until serving time. **Yield:** 9 loaves.

BUTTER DIPS
Elaine Norton, Lansing, Michigan

(PICTURED ON PAGE 74)

- 1/3 cup butter
- 2-1/2 cups flour
- 1 tablespoon sugar
- 3-1/2 teaspoons baking powder
- 1-1/2 teaspoons salt
- 1/2 to 1 cup sharp cheddar cheese, grated
- 1 cup milk

TOPPINGS:
Sesame seeds, garlic, onion, OR celery salt*

*Can use garlic, onion powders or celery seed to reduce sodium. Melt butter in 13- x 9-in. baking pan in 450° oven. Remove pan from oven when butter is melted. Set aside. In large bowl, combine flour, sugar, baking powder, salt and cheese; add milk. Stir slowly with fork. When dough clings together, turn onto well-floured board. Roll to coat with flour. Knead *gently* 10 times. Roll dough into 12- x 8-in. rectangle, 1/2 in. thick. Cut dough in half with sharp knife, then into 16 strips. Dip both sides of sticks in melted butter. Lay 2 rows in pan. Sprinkle with topping of choice. Bake at 450° for 12-15 minutes. Serve immediately. **Yield:** 32 sticks.

ALMOND TEA BREAD
Kathleen Showers, Briggsdale, Colorado

(PICTURED ON PAGE 74)

- 1 can (8 ounces) almond paste
- 1/4 cup butter, softened
- 1 cup sugar
- 3 eggs
- 1-1/2 cups fresh pitted cherries OR blueberries
- 3 cups all-purpose flour
- 4 teaspoons baking powder
- 1/2 teaspoon salt
- 3/4 cup milk

Combine almond paste and butter in large bowl; beat until well blended. Gradually add sugar, beating until light and fluffy. Add eggs, one at a time, beating well after each addition. Set aside. Combine cherries/blueberries and 1 tablespoon of flour in bowl. Toss gently to coat. Set aside. Combine the *remaining* flour, baking powder and salt. Add flour mixture to creamed mixture alternately with milk. Spoon *one-sixth* of batter into each of 2 greased and floured 7-1/2- x 3-1/2- x 3- in. loaf pans; sprinkle layers with *half of fruit.* Cover with another layer of batter and sprinkle with remaining fruit. Spoon remaining batter on top. Smooth with spatula. Bake at 350° for 1 hour and 15 minutes or until wooden pick tests clean. Cool in pan 10 minutes; remove from pan to wire rack to complete cooling.

PUMPKIN RIBBON BREAD
Cathy Van Sickel, Kokomo, Indiana

(PICTURED ON PAGE 74)

FILLING:
- 2 packages (3 ounces each) cream cheese, softened
- 1/3 cup sugar
- 1 tablespoon flour
- 1 egg
- 2 teaspoons grated orange peel

BREAD:
- 1 cup cooked pumpkin
- 1/2 cup vegetable oil
- 2 eggs
- 1-1/2 cups sugar
- 1/2 teaspoon salt
- 1/2 teaspoon cloves
- 1/2 teaspoon cinnamon
- 1-2/3 cups all-purpose flour
- 1 teaspoon baking soda
- 1 cup chopped pecans

For filling, beat cream cheese, sugar and flour together in small bowl. Add egg; mix to blend. Stir in orange peel; set aside. Make bread by combining pumpkin, oil and eggs in large bowl. Add sugar, salt, cloves, cinnamon, flour, baking soda and pecans; mix to blend. Pour *one-quarter* of batter into two greased and floured 7-1/2- x 3-1/2- x 3-in. loaf pans. Carefully spread the cream cheese mixture over batter. Add remaining batter, covering filling. Bake at 325° for 1-1/2 hours or until bread tests done with wooden pick. Cool 10 minutes before removing from pans. Store in refrigerator.

APPLE STREUSEL MUFFINS/BREAD
Cynthia Kolberg, Syracuse, Indiana

(PICTURED ON PAGE 74)

MUFFINS:
- 1-1/2 cups flour
- 1/4 cup sugar
- 2 teaspoons baking powder
- 1/2 teaspoon cinnamon
- 1/4 teaspoon salt
- 1/8 teaspoon nutmeg
- 1 cup apple, pared and shredded
- 1/2 cup milk
- 1/4 cup vegetable oil
- 1 egg, beaten

STREUSEL TOPPING:
- 1/3 cup brown sugar
- 2 tablespoons all-purpose flour
- 1/2 teaspoon cinnamon
- 2 tablespoons butter, softened
- 1/3 cup chopped pecans

In medium bowl, sift together flour, sugar, baking powder, cinnamon, salt and nutmeg. Stir in apple; set aside. In small bowl, combine milk, oil and egg until blended. Add to dry ingredients; stir just until moistened. Spoon *half* of batter into 12 greased muffin cups. Make topping by mixing together brown sugar, flour, cinnamon, butter and pecans and sprinkle on muffins, reserving 3 tablespoons. Cover each muffin with remaining half of batter. Sprinkle reserved topping on muffins. Bake at 400° for 20-25 minutes or until muffin tests done with wooden pick. Serve warm. (Recipe makes up in loaf by spooning into 8- x 4- x 2-in. loaf pan. Bake at 350° for 45-50 minutes. Cool in pan 10 minutes; remove to complete cooling on rack.) **Yield:** 12 muffins OR 1 loaf. **Diabetic Exchanges:** One serving equals 1 bread, 1 fruit, 1-1/2 fat; also, 193 calories, 149 mg sodium, 28 mg cholesterol, 25 gm carbohydrate, 3 gm protein, 8 gm fat.

LAYERED RASPBERRY SALAD
Germaine Stank, Pound, Wisconsin

- 1 package (10 ounces) frozen raspberries, thawed (reserve juice)
- 1 can (7 ounces) crushed pineapple, drained (reserve juice)
- 1 package (3 ounces) raspberry-flavor gelatin dessert

CREAM CHEESE LAYER:
- 1 envelope unflavored gelatin
- 1/4 cup cold water
- 2 packages (3 ounces *each*) cream cheese, softened
- 1 cup whipping cream
- 1/4 cup confectioners' sugar
- 1/2 cup broken pecans

Combine reserved juices from fruits and enough water to make 1-3/4 cups of liquid. Heat to boiling; pour over gelatin. Stir to dissolve; cool until partially set. Add raspberries. Pour into oiled ring mold; chill until set. For cheese layer, soak gelatin in cold water. Dissolve over hot water; cool. Cream cheese in small bowl of mixer at low speed. Add whipping cream; beat at high speed until stiff. Fold in sugar. Add cooled gelatin to pineapple; fold into whipped cream mixture. Add nuts. Pour on top of raspberry layer in mold. Refrigerate until firm. **Yield:** 10-12 servings.

HERB BUTTERS

CHIVE BUTTER:
- 1/2 cup unsalted butter, softened
- 1 teaspoon dried chives OR 1 tablespoon fresh chives

Use on noodles, crackers, chicken, white fish, corn or potatoes.

DILL BUTTER:
- 1/2 cup unsalted butter, softened
- 1/4 teaspoon dried dill weed OR 3/4 teaspoon fresh minced dill

Use on crackers, eggs, salmon, carrots, peas and zucchini. **Yield:** 1/2 cup.

STILLRIDGE CHICKEN CASSEROLE
Mary Lou Riddle, Woodstock, Maryland

- 3 cups cooked, diced chicken
- 8 ounces raw macaroni
- 2 10-3/4-ounce cans cream of mushroom soup
- 2 cups milk
- 1/2 pound sharp cheddar cheese, grated
- 1 ounce jar of pimientos, chopped
- 1/4 cup chopped green pepper
- 1 tablespoon chopped onions
- 1 teaspoon salt
- 1 teaspoon dried rosemary (or 2 teaspoons fresh)

Mix all ingredients together. Let stand overnight in refrigerator for 6-8 hours. Bake in deep, 2-quart casserole until golden brown, about 1 to 1-1/4 hours. Serve with warm bread and tossed salad.

BOUQUET GARNI

Combine 2 sprigs parsley, 2 sprigs thyme, 2 sprigs sweet marjoram with 1 bay leaf in a 6-in. square of cheesecloth; tie securely with dental floss. To use in cooking with meats, let simmer last half hour. Remove before serving. **Yield:** 1 bouquet garni.

HERB HINTS
- ● Cooking with herbs can reduce the need for salt. ● Use sprigs of fresh rosemary with your basting sauce on grilled chicken. ● Garden-ripened tomatoes are wonderful sliced, garnished with fresh chopped basil, salt and pepper and drizzled with oil. ● Use tarragon vinegar in your next chicken or potato salad dressing. ● Season green beans with a sprig of summer savory…an old German custom. ● Add herbs with a light hand …better too little than too much. ● Put a bay leaf in flour and cornmeal to prevent those little black kitchen bugs from moving in.

HERB 'N' LEMON SEASONING

Grated peel of 1/2 fresh lemon
- 2 teaspoons dried parsley flakes
- 1/2 teaspoon garlic powder
- 1/2 teaspoon dried oregano OR basil leaves, crushed
- 1/2 teaspoon dried marjoram leaves, crushed
- 1/2 teaspoon ground allspice
- 1/2 teaspoon pepper

Combine all ingredients. Refrigerate in covered container. To use, sprinkle over meat, poultry or fish before broiling or baking. **Yield:** 2 tablespoons. Free Exchange, 0 calories.

HERB-BUTTERED PASTA

- 1 7-ounce package linguine

SAUCE:
- 1/4 cup butter
- 1/3 cup chopped fresh parsley
- 1/2 teaspoon garlic powder
- 1/2 teaspoon oregano leaves
- 1 tablespoon lemon juice

Parmesan cheese

Cook linguine in 3-quart saucepan according to package instructions. Drain. Melt butter in same saucepan. Stir in linguine and remaining ingredients. Cook over medium heat, stirring constantly, until heated, about 2 minutes. Sprinkle with cheese. **Yield:** 4 servings.

SPINACH SALAD
Linda McCoy, Greensburg, Indiana

SALAD:
- 1 pound fresh spinach, washed and drained
- 2 cups fresh bean sprouts OR one No. 2 can sprouts, drained
- 1 can (8-ounce) water chestnuts, drained, sliced
- 4 hard-cooked eggs, sliced
- 1/4 cup green onions, including tops, sliced
- 1/2 pound bacon, fried, crumbled
- 1 cup fresh mushrooms, sliced

DRESSING:

- 3/4 cup sugar
- 1/4 cup vinegar
- 1/4 cup salad oil
- 1/3 cup catsup
- 2 teaspoons salt
- 1 teaspoon Worcestershire sauce

Tear clean, crisp, thoroughly dried spinach into large salad bowl. Rinse and drain sprouts. Toss all salad ingredients together. Set aside. Combine dressing ingredients in jar. Cover; shake well. Pour dressing over salad at serving time; toss lightly until spinach leaves are well-coated. Serve immediately. **Yield:** 10 servings.

LEMON SNOWDROPS
Bernice Martinoni, Petaluma, California

DOUGH:

- 1 cup butter
- 1/2 cup confectioners' sugar
- 1 teaspoon lemon extract
- 2 cups all-purpose flour
- 1/4 teaspoon salt

LEMON BUTTER FILLING:

- 1 egg, slightly beaten
- Grated rind of 1 lemon
- 2/3 cup sugar
- 3 tablespoons lemon juice
- 1-1/2 tablespoons softened butter
- Confectioners' sugar

Cream together butter and sugar; add extract. Sift flour and salt together; add to creamed mixture; mix well. Using level teaspoons of dough, form balls. Flatten slightly. Place 1 in. apart on ungreased baking sheet. Bake at 350° for 8-10 minutes. Cool. Make lemon butter filling by combining all ingredients in top of double boiler. Cook over hot water until thick, stirring constantly. Cool. Put two cookies together with filling between. Roll in confectioners' sugar. **Yield:** 2-1/2 to 3 dozen.

BUYING FRESH LEMONS

- If buying for juice, select lemons with thin, leathery rind that feels soft and juicy when gentle pressure is applied.
- If buying for rind, select lemons with thick, firm rind that feels solid when gentle pressure is applied.

AUNT MARION'S FRUIT SALAD
Marion LaTourette, Honesdale, Pennsylvania

- 1 can (11 ounces) mandarin oranges*
- 1 can (20 ounces) pineapple chunks*
- 1 can (16 ounces) peach slices*
- 3 bananas
- 2 red apples
- Fresh blueberries or raspberries, optional

FRUIT SAUCE:

- 1 box (3-3/4 ounces) *instant* vanilla pudding
- 1 cup milk
- 1/3 cup orange juice concentrate—*do not dilute*
- 3/4 cup cultured sour cream

*Fresh fruit may be substituted for canned, if desired. Drain all canned fruit well. Slice bananas; chop *unpeeled* apples and peaches into bite-sized pieces. Mix all fruit together gently; set aside. To make sauce, combine *dry* pudding with milk, orange juice concentrate and sour cream. Beat with wire whisk until smooth. (Mixture will thicken.) Mix fruit into sauce with wooden spoon. Stir well; cover; chill. **Yield:** 10 servings.

LEMON TORTE
Kristi Twohig, Oshkosh, Wisconsin

MERINGUE:

- 4 egg whites
- 1/4 teaspoon cream of tartar
- 1 cup sugar
- 1 teaspoon vanilla

CUSTARD:

- 4 egg yolks
- 2 tablespoons to 1/2 cup sugar
- 2 tablespoons lemon juice
- 2 tablespoons lemon rind

TOPPING:

- 1 pint whipping cream, whipped

Beat egg whites and cream of tartar until stiff and glossy. Gradually beat in sugar and vanilla. Spread in *well-buttered* 9- x 13-in. pan or large tart pan with removable bottom. Bake at 300° for 1 hour. Remove from oven to draft-free spot; cool thoroughly. Meanwhile, beat egg yolks until lemon-colored; add sugar, lemon juice and rind. Cook

in double boiler over low heat, stirring occasionally until thick. Cool thoroughly. Spread half of whipped cream on cooled meringue shell; cover with custard layer. Spread whipped cream over all. Refrigerate, covered. (Best if made day ahead.) **Yield:** 16 servings.

CHICKEN CORDON BLEU
Janice Thompson, Martin, Michigan

- 3 large chicken breasts, boned, skinned and halved lengthwise, about 1-1/2 pounds
- 6 thin slices boiled ham
- 6 thin slices Swiss cheese
- 2 tablespoons butter
- 1 can (10-3/4 ounces) cream of mushroom soup
- 2 tablespoons milk OR white wine
- 1 can (2-1/2 to 3 ounces) sliced mushrooms, drained
- 1 tablespoon minced parsley

Pound chicken breasts with mallet until 1/4 in. thick. Place 1 slice ham and 1 slice cheese on each. Tuck in sides and roll up jelly-roll fashion. Skewer with two toothpicks; set aside. Melt butter in microwave in 8- x 12-in. glass baking dish. Microwave breasts in melted butter on HIGH 3 minutes, uncovered. Turn chicken over so seam side is down; microwave on HIGH for 3 minutes. Combine soup with milk (or wine) and mushrooms. Pour over chicken. Cover with waxed paper. Microwave on HIGH 7 minutes, rotating dish after 3-1/2 minutes. Garnish with minced parsley. **Yield:** 6 servings.

MICROWAVE TIPS

- *Converting a recipe to microwave?* Compare it to a similar microwave recipe. As a general rule, you can cut the cooking time down to 1/3 to 1/4 of the total conventional time. Test for doneness; add time as needed in small amounts.
- *What power level for what?* Fruits, vegetables, fish and poultry can use HIGH power. Use 70% POWER for tender meats and casseroles, 50% POWER for less-tender cuts of meat. ● *What foods work best?* Microwave ovens provide a *moist* method of cooking. Dishes that use liquids (one-pot meals, soups, casseroles) work well. (You can often reduce the liquid called for in a conventional recipe by 1/3.) Check food during cooking; add moisture as needed.

Country Inns

The Wildflower Inn
Star Route, Lyndonville, Vermont 05851, 802/626-8310

Directions: Take Exit 23 off I-91 at Lyndonville. Follow US 5 north through town to Hwy. 114. Right on 114 for 1/2 mile; turn left immediately following second bridge. Continue 2 miles to inn.

Schedule: Open year-round except for short periods in April and November. Full breakfast 8:30-9:30 a.m. (7:30 a.m winter for skiers) and afternoon tea (beverages and homemade goodies) served 4 to 5:30 p.m. to inn guests. Barbecue grills and kitchen utensils available for use.

Accommodations: 4 rooms with 2 shared baths in farmhouse, 11 rooms with private baths in carriage barn. Smoking in designated areas only.

Hours and rates subject to change. Please call or write.

BREAKFAST specialties are part of the appeal of the Wildflower Inn—including gingercakes with applesauce and whipped cream...blueberry muffins...or bacon-wrapped baked eggs. And afternoon tea—with homemade treats, local cheese and fresh fruit—is the perfect way to unwind after an outdoors day. Try some of these recipes yourself:

WILDFLOWER INN BLUEBERRY MUFFINS

   1 cup unbleached white flour
1/2 cup whole wheat flour
1/2 cup brown sugar
1/2 cup wheat germ
   1 tablespoon baking powder
1/2 teaspoon salt
1/2 cup butter, melted
3/4 cup milk
   2 large eggs
1/2 teaspoon vanilla
1-1/2 cups blueberries, fresh *or* frozen
Cinnamon sugar

Mix together flours, sugar, wheat germ, baking powder and salt; set aside. In separate bowl, mix melted butter (slightly cooled) with milk, eggs and vanilla. Add to dry ingredients and stir until moistened. Add berries, stirring only to distribute. Spoon batter into greased muffin cups filling two-thirds full; sprinkle with cinnamon sugar. Bake at 425° for about 15 minutes. **Yield:** 12 muffins.

MRS. NEE'S DUTCH CAKE (No Eggs)

   2 cups sugar
1/2 cup butter
   3 cups flour
   4 teaspoons baking powder
Pinch salt
   1 teaspoon vanilla
   2 cups milk

GLAZE:
1/2 cup butter
   1 tablespoon sugar
   1 teaspoon cinnamon

Mix together sugar and butter until light and fluffy. Add flour, baking powder, salt, vanilla and milk; mixing to blend. Spread in greased and floured 13-in. x 9-in. x 2-in. baking pan. Bake at 350° for about 35 minutes. Combine glaze ingredients in small saucepan until sugar dissolves. Spread over warm cake. **Yield:** 12-16 servings.

APPLE CRISP

   4 cups peeled, sliced tart apples
1/2 cup water (for less juicy apples)

TOPPING:
3/4 cup flour
   1 cup brown sugar
   1 teaspoon cinnamon
1/2 cup softened butter
1/4 teaspoon salt
3/4 cup old-fashioned *or* quick cooking oats
Whipped cream *or* ice cream

Butter a deep baking dish; fill with apples and water; set aside. Combine topping ingredients until crumbly; sprinkle over apple filling. Bake at 350° for about 30 minutes. Serve with whipped cream or ice cream. **Yield:** 6 servings.

MARSHA BARS

   2 cups brown sugar
   1 cup butter, softened
   3 eggs
1-1/2 teaspoons vanilla
   2 cups flour
1/2 teaspoon baking soda
1/2 teaspoon salt
   1 cup ground almonds
   1 cup coconut
1-1/2 cups semisweet chocolate chips

Place sugar, butter, eggs and vanilla in large mixing bowl; mix well until fluffy. Set aside. In separate bowl, toss together flour, soda, salt, almonds, coconut and chips. Mix into first mixture with spoon. Spread in greased 13-in. x 9-in. x 2-in. baking pan. Bake at 350° for 30 minutes. Cool; cut into bars. **Yield:** 32 1-1/2-in. sq. bars.

PRIZE-WINNING baked goods are a specialty of Fancheon Resler, who's from Goshen, Indiana. She's won many competitions, including the Indiana Archway Cookie Contest at the State Fair. But more than that, her thoughtfulness makes her the "Best Cook in the Country", according to her friend Patricia Franke of Wolcottville, Indiana.

Patricia wrote, "Fancheon is a dynamic, thoughtful woman...well-known for giving away hundreds of food items each year, for birthdays, Christmas, get-well remembrances, funeral meals...and sometimes just to brighten someone else's day."

APRICOT RING-A-LINGS

DOUGH:
- 2 packages active dry yeast
- 1/2 cup warm water
- 1/3 cup sugar
- 2/3 cup softened butter, *divided*
- 2 teaspoons salt
- 2/3 cup scalded milk
- 2 unbeaten eggs
- 4-1/2 to 5 cups all purpose flour

FILLING:
- 1 cup confectioners' sugar
- 1 cup finely chopped pecans
- Apricot preserves

Soften yeast in warm water. Combine sugar, 1/3 cup butter, salt and milk in large mixing bowl. Cool to lukewarm; stir in eggs and yeast. Add flour to form stiff dough. On lightly floured surface, knead until smooth and satiny. Place in greased bowl; cover. Let rise 1-1/2 hours. Combine confectioners' sugar, remaining butter and pecans. Roll out one-half of dough to form 12-in. x 12-in. square. Spread one-half

Illus. 1

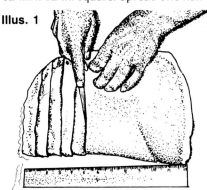

of apricot mixture over half of dough. Fold uncovered dough over filling and pinch edges together. Cut into 1-inch strips. (Illustration 1.) Twist each strip

Illus. 2

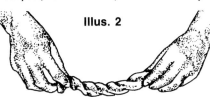

4 or 5 times, holding carefully. (Illustration 2.) Hold down one end on greased baking sheet to form center of

Illus. 3

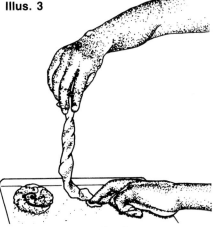

roll. (Illustration 3.) Curl remaining strip around center as for pinwheel; tuck end under. Indent center and fill with 1/2 teaspoon apricot preserves. Repeat with other one-half of dough and filling. Cover; let rise 45 minutes. Bake at 375° for 18 minutes or until lightly browned. Glaze with confec-

tioners' sugar glaze, if desired. **Yield.** 24 pastries.

RHUBARB DREAM BARS

CRUST:
- 2 cups flour
- 3/4 cup confectioners' sugar
- 1 cup butter *or* margarine

FILLING:
- 4 eggs
- 2 cups sugar
- 1/2 cup flour
- 1/2 teaspoon salt
- 4 cups thinly sliced fresh rhubarb

Mix crust ingredients together; press into 15-in. x 10-in. pan. Bake at 350° for 15 minutes (crust will be very light-colored).Combine eggs, sugar, flour and salt; beat together. Fold in rhubarb. Spread filling mixture on hot crust; return to oven to bake 40 to 45 minutes longer. Cool; cut into bars. **Yield:** 36 bars.

JUST RIGHT CHOCOLATE CHIP COOKIES

- 2/3 cup butter *or* margarine
- 2/3 cup butter-flavored solid shortening
- 3/4 cup white sugar
- 3/4 cup brown sugar, packed
- 2 eggs
- 2 teaspoons real vanilla extract
- 3 cups flour
- 1 teaspoon baking soda
- 1 teaspoon salt
- 1 package (3-1/2 ounces) *instant* vanilla pudding mix
- 1 package (12 ounces) semisweet chocolate chips

With mixer, beat shortenings together until fluffy. Add both sugars; beat until well-blended. Beat in eggs and vanilla. Set aside. In separate bowl, mix together flour, soda, salt and pudding mix. Gradually add to beaten mixture, stirring well. Stir in chocolate chips. Drop by heaping tablespoonsful onto ungreased cookie sheet. Bake at 350° for 14-18 minutes. (Longer baking time yields a crunchier cookie; less time a chewy one.) **Yield:** 4 dozen cookies.

HURRAY for holiday hospitality! Polish the pewter, deck the halls and set out a tempting array for a family gathering or neighborhood open house!

These appealing buffet dishes are favorites for festive feasts—sure to add to holiday enjoyment.

Begin with appetizers...tasty Shrimp Curry Dip with colorful crudites...hot Cheese Snack Crackers studded with ripe olives...or a buttery, savory Cheddar Cheese Spread.

Round out the feast with two rich seafood chowders, a jeweled cranberry mold and a fresh, refreshing holiday fruit salad. And, for an ambrosial ending, bring on the creamy Scandinavian Rice Pudding!

HOLIDAY HOSPITALITY: Counterclockwise from lower right—Shrimp Curry Dip (Pg. 93); Wisconsin Cheddar Cheese Spread (Pg. 92); Creamy Rice Pudding (Pg. 92); Cranberry Supreme Salad (Pg. 92); Salmon Chowder (Pg. 92); Oyster Chowder (Pg. 92); Holiday Fruit Salad (Pg. 92); Wheat/Cheese Snack Crackers (Pg. 92).

Pewter Courtesy of The Red Fox, Mequon, Wisconsin

HOLIDAY traditions aren't complete without ethnic yeast breads. Every country cook hoards a treasured family recipe passed down through the generations.

The very special sweet baked holiday treats here include prune and apricot Kolache from Czechoslovakia...light, sweet Kringla from Scandinavia...almond-flavored Bonket from the Netherlands... and nut- and fruit-laden Almond Braid—a favorite in many cultures.

Keep old traditions alive—or start a brand-new one—with these delicious, satisfying yeast breads.

OLD WORLD FAVORITES: Clockwise from lower left—Almond Braid (Pg. 94); Kringla (Pg. 93); Kolache (Pg. 93); Bonket (Dutch Letters) (Pg. 93).

Holiday Favorites

HOLIDAYS can be hurried days in country homes, with special meals and lots of entertaining taking up precious time.

To help get you through the holiday season, we've collected some tried-and-true and some fresh-and-new holiday recipes...plenty of ideas for homemade gift-giving...and a roundup of helpful hints and suggestions to make the holiday season less of a burden and more of a joy.

On this and the following two pages, you'll find suggestions...recipes are on pages 92-95.

And *happy holidays* from *our* country kitchen to *yours!*

HOLIDAY CLASSICS: Clockwise from left—Sweet Yeast Rolls (Pg. 94); Red Cabbage with Apples (Pg. 94); Pepparkakor (Pg. 94); Mulled Apple Cider (Pg. 94); Apricot Kolache (Pg. 95); Goose stuffed with Apple Raisin Stuffing (Pg. 95).

TESTED HOLIDAY TIPS:

● Check oven temperatures of dishes for compatibility. If temperatures vary, think of preparing some dishes in your microwave.

● Consider texture in meal planning. Balance soft foods (such as a potato or squash dish) with the crunch of a salad or a crisply cooked vegetable.

● Remember dieters and those on low-sodium, low-sugar, low-fat diets at your table as you plan your meals. Use less salt in food preparation—those who wish more can add it at the table. Always serve some pretty, fresh fruit for diabetics, in addition to those richer desserts.

Reduce fats in food preparation wherever you can, too. For instance, use 1 tablespoon of oil for sauteing instead of 2.

● Don't try to prepare all the dishes yourself...you'll end up overworked and overtired! Many holiday gatherings lend themselves to the potluck format—suggest a dish to cooks who volunteer and let the noncooks bring salad greens, relish plates, cheese plates or a basket of fresh fruit.

Crowd-pleasing Christmas Dishes

FESTIVE HOLIDAY FOOD: Clockwise from top right—Fresh Fruit with Orange Cheese Dip (Pg. 95); Rhubarb Strawberry Salad (Pg. 95); Overnight Danish Braid (Pg. 95) and Chocolate Ladies (Pg. 95).

CHRISTMAS in the country means company for dinner...boots in the front hall...pies on the back porch ...and concern over whether we'll have enough clean forks for dessert!

In a word, a country Christmas means people...wall-to-wall people and enough good food to feed the crowds of family and friends that typify our holiday season.

With that in mind, we've collected a full measure of crowd-pleasing recipes (starting on page 92) for you and your family and friends to enjoy during this joyous season...and whenever else good people and good food get together.

Here's a suggested holiday menu that is certain to please guests and win compliments for the cook. Choose one of your own favorite potato dishes to complete the menu. (Potatoes Ro-manoff on page 75 is a good choice, as well).

Mulled Apple Cider, p. 94
Goose stuffed with Apple
   Raisin Stuffing, p. 95
Red Cabbage with Apples, p. 94
Rhubarb Strawberry Salad, p. 95
Sweet Yeast Rolls, p. 94
Fresh Fruit with Orange
   Cheese Dip, p. 95
Pepparkakor Cookies, p. 94
Chocolate Ladies, p. 95

Gifts from the Kitchen

THE BEST Christmas gifts come from the heart and the hands of a country cook...just ask the lucky recipient!

Spicy or sweet...crunchy, nutty or deliciously rich, holiday gifts from your kitchen make everyone smile. Packaged in imaginative ways, these treats are even more fun to give and to receive.

Here are some pretty, practical suggestions for presenting your food gifts.

● Save jars with unusual shapes (instant coffee jars are nice). To remove prices from jar lids, use nail polish remover.

● Buy wooden lids (available at grocery/department stores) for recycled jars.

● Tie a sprig of fresh evergreen and bright ribbon around each jar top. Buy Christmas decals/stickers to decorate plain lids.

● Save small cans that come with plastic lids (cover with red or green felt or Con-Tact paper).

● Cover the tops of clean egg cartons with Christmas fabric; line each cup with colored paper liners—just right for special candies!

● Use Stitch Witchery to make fabric gift tags and labels.

● Print or type instructions for food gifts. Be sure your label tells how to store the food. (Refrigerate? Store covered?)

● Collect crocks, baskets and tins throughout the year so you'll have plenty on hand when gift-giving season arrives.

Focus Is Food at Molly Stark House

FOOD plays a leading role at the Molly Stark House—not only as nourishment for the bed and breakfast guests, but also in the inn's cooking school, wedding receptions and celebrations and in the private, candlelight dinners Jim and Ellie Manser prepare on weekends for two to 40.

A sample menu from one of their weekend dinners—this a group of 28—gives an indication of the care

The Molly Stark House
Page's Corner, R.D. 2,
Dunbarton NH 03301,
603/774-4402
Jim and Ellie Manser, Innkeepers

and imagination which go into all their cooking: an onion/filo roll appetizer, Beef Stroganoff with Noodles, Baked Herb Chicken (using herbs straight from their garden),

potato salad, green salad with creamy mustard dressing, whole wheat French bread, ratatouille, fresh strawberry cream roll, coffee ice cream cake, chocolate sour cream layer cake and rhubarb pie.

Yes, four desserts! Ellie tries to have at least four for each dinner. She and Jim split the cooking—if he does the beef and duckling entrees, she does the seafood. He bakes bread

...she makes potato salad. He arranges a fruit cascade...she does appetizers.

The Mansers bought the Molly Stark House 5 years ago and have been renovating it ever since, careful to maintain and restore the architectural heritage of the 232-year-old house, with its Moses Eaton stenciled walls and random-width plank floors. They turned the attached carriage house into a gift shop and cooking school.

The inn also houses their collections: Ellie's 400-volume cookbook collection, yellowware bowls, cream and water pitchers, baskets and clear Depression glass pedestal plates and Jim's old bird houses and wooden planes.

Whether guests at the Molly Stark House savor breakfast on the sun porch or in the keeping room, enjoy hors d'ouevres in the parlor...dinner in the formal dining room...or an outdoor buffet served in the gazebo, they leave with beautiful memories of the food and the surroundings—so evocative of simpler, more restful times.

ORIENTAL WING DINGS

24 chicken wings, disjointed

MARINADE:
1/2 cup light soy sauce
1/2 cup white wine
1 teaspoon minced garlic
2 tablespoons vegetable oil
Seasoned crumbs
Melted butter

Combine marinade; add chicken wings and marinate up to one day, covered, in refrigerator. Drain wings; bake at 400° for 20 minutes. Cool until easy to handle. Roll in seasoned crumbs; brush with melted butter. Bake for 10 more minutes at 400° until brown.

GREAT PUFFY PANCAKE

1/2 cup flour
1/2 cup milk
2 eggs, slightly beaten
Pinch nutmeg
4 tablespoons butter

2 tablespoons confectioners' sugar
Juice of 1/2 lemon

Mix flour, milk, eggs and nutmeg together (mixture will be slightly lumpy). Melt butter in large cast iron frying pan. Add batter. Bake at 425° for 15-20 minutes or until golden brown. Sprinkle with sugar and lemon juice. Cut into wedges. **Yield:** 4 servings.

CHILLED SUMMER SQUASH SOUP

3 summer squash (1-1/2 pounds)
1 tablespoon butter
4 green onions, chopped
1-1/2 cups chicken broth
Salt
Fresh ground white pepper
Pinch nutmeg
1 cup light cream
2 tablespoons snipped chives
Croutons

Scrub squash well, leaving skins intact. Slice or cut into chunks. Melt butter in large saucepan; saute onions until tender. Add squash and broth; cover, cook until squash is tender, about 15 minutes. Puree mixture in blender or food processor. Transfer to a bowl. Season with salt, pepper and nutmeg. Stir in cream; chill. Serve very cold with snipped chives and croutons. **Yield:** 6 servings.

VEAL MARSALA

1/2 cup all-purpose flour
Salt
Freshly ground black pepper
6 tablespoons butter
1 pound veal, thinly sliced and pounded
1 medium onion, finely chopped
4 to 5 tablespoons chopped fresh parsley
Juice of a 1/2 lemon, approximately 2 tablespoons
1/2 pound fresh mushrooms, sliced
1/2 cup dry Marsala wine
1 cup beef broth

Mix flour, salt and pepper in bowl. Heat butter in skillet. Dip both sides of veal in flour mixture; shake off excess. (Dip in flour as you cook them to prevent

flour from becoming soggy and browning poorly.) When butter stops foaming, add veal. Brown quickly on both sides. Saute *only* as many pieces at a time as will fit in a single layer. Transfer veal to warmed platter. Add onions to skillet; cook until soft. Add parsley, lemon juice and mushrooms. Cook several minutes more. Add wine and broth and any of juices that have collected from meat. Boil briskly until sauce is reduced and thickened, scraping up brown bits from bottom of pan. Reduce heat to very low. Add veal, basting with sauce once or twice. Transfer meat and sauce to platter and serve at once. **Yield:** 4 servings.

LEMON CHEESECAKE

(With Blueberry/Spice Topping)

CHEESECAKE:
1/4 cup melted butter
1-1/2 cups graham cracker crumbs
1-3/4 cups sugar, *divided*
3 packages (8 ounces each) cream cheese, softened
4 eggs
1/4 cup lemon juice
3/4 teaspoon vanilla extract

BLUEBERRY/SPICE TOPPING:
1/2 cup sugar
1 tablespoon cornstarch
1/2 teaspoon ground cinnamon
1/4 teaspoon ground nutmeg
1/4 cup hot water
2 tablespoons lemon juice
2 cups fresh *or* dry pack frozen blueberries

In small bowl, combine butter, crumbs and *1/4 cup sugar.* Pat firmly on bottom of 9-inch springform pan. In large mixer bowl, beat cheese until fluffy. Beat in remaining sugar and eggs until smooth. Add lemon juice and vanilla, mixing on low speed until well-blended. Pour into prepared pan. Bake at 300° for 1 hour and 5-10 minutes or until cake springs back when lightly touched. Carefully loosen top of cheesecake from edge of pan with knife tip. Cool to room temperature; chill. Make topping by combining sugar, cornstarch, cinnamon and nutmeg in small pan; gradually stir in water and lemon juice. Over medium heat, cook until mixture thickens and comes to boil. Add blueberries; cook and stir until mixture returns to a boil. Spoon sauce over cheesecake; chill for about 15 minutes before serving. **Yield:** 12 servings.

OYSTER CHOWDER
Beverly Anderson, Sinclairville, New York

(PICTURED ON PAGE 84)

12 ounces fresh shucked oysters with liquor (oyster liquid) (canned may be substituted but omit salt)
1 coarsely chopped onion, about 1/2 cup
1 medium potato, diced
1 cup coarsely cut broccoli
1/2 cup frozen corn

CHOWDER BASE:
1/4 cup butter
1/4 cup flour
1 cup chicken broth
3 cups milk
Salt to taste
White pepper to taste

Heat oysters in liquor in pan until edges curl; set aside. Combine onion, potato, broccoli and corn in saucepan with 1 cup water; simmer until tender. Set aside. Make white sauce by melting butter in pan, stir in flour. Cook, stirring, for one minute. Add broth and milk gradually; cook until mixture thickens. Add reserved oyster liquor and vegetables. Heat through—DO NOT BOIL. Add seasoning to taste. **Yield:** 6-8 servings.

SALMON CHOWDER
Linda Fox, Soldotna, Alaska

(PICTURED ON PAGE 84)

4 tablespoons butter OR margarine
1 medium onion, chopped
1 cup water
1 package (20 ounces) frozen chopped broccoli
1 can (16 ounces) red salmon, bones and skin removed
2 teaspoons instant chicken bouillon granules
1 can (14-1/2 ounces) evaporated milk
2 tablespoons flour
4 cups milk
Salt to taste
White pepper

Saute onion in butter in Dutch oven until transparent. Add water and broccoli; simmer until broccoli is tender. Add salmon, instant chicken bouillon granules, *evaporated milk and flour* (which have been mixed together) and milk. Season with salt and pepper to

taste. Heat until mixture thickens slightly. **Yield:** 8 servings.

HOLIDAY FRUIT SALAD
Margaret Allen, Abingdon, Virginia

(PICTURED ON PAGE 84)

1 can (15-1/2 ounces) pineapple chunks, *reserve juice*
1/2 cup sugar
2 tablespoons all-purpose flour
1 egg, beaten
1 cup pecans, chopped
3 bananas, sliced
2 cans (11 ounces *each*) mandarin oranges, drained
3 medium unpeeled apples, chopped
1/2 pound red seedless grapes, *halved*

Drain pineapple; place juice in small saucepan. Add sugar, flour and egg to juice; cook over low heat, stirring constantly until smooth and thickened. Cool. Combine pecans and fruit; add dressing, stirring well. Chill before serving. **Yield:** 10-12 servings.

WHEAT/CHEESE SNACK CRACKERS
Rosemarie Starr, Hillman, Minnesota

(PICTURED ON PAGE 84)

1 box (13 ounces) shredded wheat snack crackers

CHEESE SPREAD:
1-1/2 cups mayonnaise, *no substitutes*
2 cups mozzarella cheese, shredded
2 cups cheddar cheese, shredded
1 can (4-1/4 ounces) chopped ripe olives
6 green onions, sliced 1/8-in. thick

Place crackers, edges touching, on cookie sheet. Mix cheese spread ingredients; spread on crackers. Bake at 250° for 20 minutes. Serve hot. **Yield:** 5 dozen.

WISCONSIN CHEDDAR CHEESE SPREAD
Patricia Hazen, Brookfield, Wisconsin

(PICTURED ON PAGE 85)

1 pound grated sharp cheddar cheese
1 cup chopped walnuts
1 cup mayonnaise
1/4 cup finely diced green onion
1/2 teaspoon curry powder
Dash Tabasco sauce
Crackers

Combine all ingredients; mix well. Pack into crocks; refrigerate until firm. Serve with assorted crackers. **Yield:** 24 servings.

CRANBERRY SUPREME SALAD
Gertrude Zelepuza, Aberdeen, Washington

(PICTURED ON PAGE 85)

1 package (3 ounces) raspberry gelatin dessert
1 cup boiling water
1 can (16 ounces) whole cranberry sauce
1 package (3 ounces) lemon gelatin dessert
1 cup boiling water
1 package (3 ounces) cream cheese
1/3 cup mayonnaise
1 can (8-1/2 ounces) crushed pineapple, *undrained*
1 cup whipping cream
1 cup miniature marshmallows

Dissolve raspberry gelatin in 1 cup boiling water; stir in cranberry sauce. Pour into bottom of a *1-1/2 qt. round* mold. Chill until partially set. Dissolve lemon gelatin in 1 cup boiling water; set aside. Beat together cream cheese and mayonnaise; gradually add lemon gelatin. Stir in pineapple. Chill until partially set. Whip cream; fold into lemon mixture, add marshmallows. Spread lemon layer on top of cranberry mixture. Chill until set. **Yield:** 12 servings.

CREAMY RICE PUDDING
Jeannette Mortenson, Albert Lea, Minnesota

(PICTURED ON PAGE 85)

6 cups milk (2% or whole)
1 cup long grain white rice
1/2 cup raisins, if desired
1 cup heavy (whipping) cream
3 beaten egg yolks

2 teaspoons vanilla
1/4 teaspoon salt
1/2 cup sugar
Cinnamon

Combine milk and rice in heavy saucepan; bring to boil. Reduce heat; simmer for 55 minutes. Combine cream, egg yolks, vanilla, salt and sugar and raisins, if desired, add to cooked rice mixture. Cook over moderate heat, stirring until thick. Pour into 2-1/2 qt. serving dish; sprinkle top with cinnamon. Serve warm, or cover and store in refrigerator. **Yield:** 10 servings.

SHRIMP CURRY DIP
Bob Fithian, Fountain Hills, Arizona

(PICTURED ON PAGE 85)

1 can (4-1/2 ounces) tiny shrimp pieces
1-1/3 cups mayonnaise
1 teaspoon TO 1 tablespoon honey
2 tablespoons catsup
1 medium onion, diced fine
2 teaspoons lemon juice
1 teaspoon tarragon vinegar
1 to 1-1/2 teaspoons curry powder
Dash tabasco sauce
Salt
Pepper
Assorted washed fresh vegetables—broccoli flowerettes, pepper strips, carrot sticks, scallions.

Combine all ingredients except assorted fresh vegetables; mix; refrigerate overnight. Serve cold with vegetables. (This also makes an excellent salad dressing thinned with milk.)

KRINGLA
Dotty Egge, Pelican Rapids, Minnesota

(PICTURED ON PAGE 86)

1-1/2 cups milk, *scalded and cooled*
2 packages active dry yeast
1/2 cup warm water (110-115°)
1 cup sugar
2 eggs
1/2 cup vegetable shortening
1-1/4 teaspoons salt
About 7 cups all-purpose flour
1/2 cup soft butter

Heat milk to about 180° in saucepan or in microwave; cool. Set aside. Dissolve yeast in warm water in large bowl;

add milk to yeast mixture. Add sugar, eggs, shortening, salt and *one half of flour;* mix well. Add remaining flour. Let rise until double; punch down. Let rise again. Form into Kringla by dividing dough in one-half. Set one-half aside. Cut into 18 pieces; roll each into 10-in.-long pencil shape. Join in a circle; twist to form a figure 8. Place on cookie sheets. Let rise until double. Bake at 350° for 10 minutes or until very light golden brown. Remove from oven; brush with butter. **Yield:** 36.

KOLACHE
Judy Holub, San Antonio, Texas

(PICTURED ON PAGE 86)

1-1/2 cups warm milk
1-1/2 packages active dry yeast
1/2 cup butter
1/2 cup sugar
1 teaspoon salt
2 egg yolks
4-1/2 cups flour

APRICOT FILLING:
6 ounces dried apricots
3/4 cup sugar
1 tablespoon melted butter
Drop almond flavoring

PRUNE FILLING:
1-1/2 cups dried pitted prunes
1/4 cup sugar
1/2 teaspoon cinnamon

CRUMBLY TOPPING:
1/4 cup flour
1/4 cup sugar
2 tablespoons softened butter
1 teaspoon cinnamon, optional

Dissolve yeast in *1/2 cup warm milk;* set aside. Heat remaining milk with butter until butter dissolves. Remove from heat; add sugar, salt and stir until dissolved. When mixture is cooled, add egg yolks; stir well. Add yeast mixture. Add flour slowly until a medium stiff dough results. Knead until smooth; place dough in large oiled bowl. Cover with towel; place in warm location un-

til dough doubles in size. Make Apricot Filling by cooking apricots in saucepan with enough water to cover. Cover pan; boil until tender. Drain; add remaining ingredients. Set aside. Make Prune Filling by cooking prunes in saucepan in enough water to cover. Cook until tender; drain. Mash with fork; stir in sugar and cinnamon. Set aside. Turn dough onto floured surface; roll out 1/4- to 1/2-in. thickness. Cut with biscuit cutter or 3-in. round glass. Place on greased cookie sheet 1-1/2 in. apart. Let rise until double in size. When kolache has doubled in size, make indentation in center of each with fingers; place 1 tablespoon filling in indentation. Top with crumb topping. Bake at 400° for 12 minutes. Cool on wire rack. (This is a slow-rising dough.) **Yield:** 30 kolaches.

BONKET (Dutch Letters)
Edna Hoffman, Hebron, Indiana

(PICTURED ON PAGE 86)

DOUGH:
4 cups unbleached flour
1 pound butter
1 cup ice water

FILLING:
1 pound almond paste
3 eggs
1/4 teaspoon almond extract
1-1/2 cups sugar

TOPPING:
Egg white
Sugar

Cut butter into flour in large bowl as for pastry; add water, gradually forming dough. Cover well; chill overnight. Prepare filling in advance by combining all ingredients (if almond paste is dry and stiff; grate it), cover mixture and chill overnight. Divide dough into 8-10 pieces; roll out on floured waxed paper to 6-in. x 18-in. rectangle on floured board. Keep unrolled dough chilled. Divide filling into equal number of portions. Place filling along *long side of roll;* fold edge over filling; roll up. Cut into shorter lengths or letter shapes, if desired. Place on greased cookie sheets. Punch holes in roll every 1 to 2 in. with round wooden skewer. Brush with slightly beaten egg white; sprinkle with sugar. Bake at 375° for 25-30 minutes. Watch carefully—do not overbake. These freeze well. Dough and filling can be kept in refrigerator several days, too. **Yield:** 18 bonkets (5 to 6 in.).

ALMOND BRAID
Karen King, Redding, California

(PICTURED ON PAGE 86)

1/2 cup milk, scalded
1/2 cup butter
1/2 cup sugar
1 teaspoon salt
2 packages active dry yeast
1/2 cup warm water (110-115°)
2 eggs, slightly beaten
5-1/2 to 5-3/4 cups all-purpose flour
1/2 candied mixed fruit
1/2 cup chopped blanched almonds

ALMOND FILLING:
1 cup finely chopped blanched almonds
1/2 cup sugar
6 tablespoons butter, melted
Almond extract, optional

GLAZE:
1 cup confectioners' sugar
2-4 tablespoons warm milk
1 tablespoon butter

Combine milk, butter, sugar and salt in large bowl; stir until butter is melted. Cool to lukewarm; set aside. Sprinkle yeast into water; let stand for 5 minutes. Stir until dissolved. Add yeast mixture and eggs to milk; mix well. Stir in 2 cups flour (combined with fruit and almonds); beat well. Add enough remaining flour to make soft dough; mix well. Turn out on lightly floured surface; knead until smooth and elastic, about 8-10 minutes. Place in a greased bowl, turning once to grease top. Cover with damp towel. Let rise in warm place until double in bulk, about 2 hours. Punch down; let rise again until doubled, about 30 minutes. Turn out on lightly floured surface. Divide dough in half; roll each into 9- x 18-in. rectangle. Make filling by combining all ingredients. Spread filling down center one-third of each rectangle. With kitchen shears, cut sides toward center in strips 3 in. long and 1 in. wide (Fig. 1). Fold strips over filling, alternating from side to side (Fig. 2). Place on greased cookie sheet; let rise until doubled. Bake at 350° for 30 to 35 minutes. Cool on wire rack. Make glaze by combining all ingredients;

drizzle over coffeecakes. **Yield:** 2 medium braids or 1 large, as shown in photo.

SWEET YEAST ROLLS
Peggy Bjorkman, Milwaukee, Wisconsin

(PICTURED ON PAGE 87)

3/5 ounce cake of compressed yeast OR 1 package active dry yeast
1/2 cup warm water
2 cups milk
1/2 cup sugar
8 cups all-purpose flour
1/2 cup melted butter
2 eggs
2 teaspoons salt

Soften yeast in warm water with a teaspoon of sugar. Scald milk; cool to lukewarm. Add yeast, sugar and enough flour to make a medium batter. Beat thoroughly. Let stand until light and foamy. Add melted butter (which has been cooled), eggs and salt. Beat well. Add enough flour to form soft dough. Sprinkle small amount of flour on counter and let dough rest. Meanwhile, clean and dry bowl; grease clean surface of bowl. Knead dough until smooth and satiny. Put in greased bowl; turn over to grease top. Cover; let rise in warm place until double in bulk. Punch down. Turn out on floured board. Divide into portions for shaping; let rest 10 minutes. Shape dough into desired forms. Place on greased baking sheets. Let rise until doubled. Bake at 375° for 10 minutes; reduce temperature to 350° for 10-15 minutes more. Cool on rack. **Yield:** 5-6 dozen rolls.

RED CABBAGE WITH APPLES
Grace Howaniec, Waukesha, Wisconsin

(PICTURED ON PAGE 87)

1 medium head red cabbage, cut in 1/8-inch strips
2 medium apples, pared, cored and cut in 1/8-inch thick slices
1/2 cup chopped onion
2 tablespoons butter
1/2 cup red wine vinegar
1 bay leaf
1 tablespoon sugar
1/2 teaspoon salt

Cook cabbage, apples and onion in butter in large skillet over medium heat for 5 minutes, stirring often. Add vinegar, bay leaf, sugar and salt. Bring mixture to boil. Reduce heat; cover. Simmer for 35 minutes or until cabbage is tender. **Yield:** 10 servings. **Diabetic Exchanges:** One serving equals 1 vegetable, 1/2 fruit, 1/2 fat; also, 70 calories, 163 mg sodium, 7 mg cholesterol, 12 gm carbohydrate.

MULLED APPLE CIDER
Grace Howaniec, Waukesha, Wisconsin

(PICTURED ON PAGE 87)

1 gallon natural apple cider*
3 sticks whole cinnamon
6 whole allspice
1 whole red apple
Whole cloves

*If possible, use freshly pressed apple cider that requires refrigeration; it will be thicker and tastier than most store brands. Place cider in large kettle; add cinnamon and allspice. Simmer over low heat for 30 minutes. Add apple, studded with cloves, about 10 minutes before serving. **Yield:** 30 4-oz. servings. **Diabetic Exchanges:** One serving equals 1-1/2 fruits; also 64 calories, 1 mg sodium, 0 cholesterol, 16 gm carbohydrate.

PEPPARKAKOR
Grace Howaniec, Waukesha, Wisconsin

(PICTURED ON PAGE 87)

1 cup butter (no substitutes)
1-1/2 cups sugar
1 tablespoon dark molasses
1 egg
3-1/4 cups all-purpose flour
2 teaspoons baking soda
1 tablespoon ground cinnamon
1 tablespoon ground ginger
1 tablespoon ground cloves
Juice and grated rind of 1 orange

(Note: Spice amount is correct.) Cream butter with sugar until light and fluffy; add syrup and egg. Mix until blended. Sift flour, soda and spices into creamed mixture. Add orange juice/rind; mix until blended. Roll dough on lightly floured board to 1/8 in. thickness. Cut into shapes (hearts, reindeer). Transfer to greased cookie sheets. Bake at 350° until brown, about 10-12 minutes. Cool on rack; store covered. **Yield:** 3-4 dozen cookies.

Fig. 1   Fig. 2

APPLE/RAISIN STUFFING
Grace Howaniec, Waukesha, Wisconsin

(PICTURED ON PAGE 87)

- 3 cups toasted bread cubes
- 1-1/2 cups chopped apples (unpared)
- 1/2 cup raisins
- 1/2 cup celery, chopped
- 1/2 cup onion, chopped
- 1 teaspoon salt
- 1/2 teaspoon sage, crumbled
- 1/4 teaspoon rosemary, crumbled
- 1/4 teaspoon ground pepper
- 1 chicken bouillon cube
- 1/2 cup hot water

Mix together bread cubes, apple, raisins, celery, onion, salt and seasonings. Dissolve bouillon cube in hot water; add to stuffing mixture. Toss lightly to mix. **Yield:** 6 cups stuffing.

APRICOT KOLACHE
Grace Howaniec, Waukesha, Wisconsin

(PICTURED ON PAGE 87)

- 1 pound butter, room temperature (no substitutes)
- 1 8-ounce package cream cheese
- 2 cups all-purpose flour
- 1 12-ounce can apricot filling

Confectioners' sugar

Mix butter and cream cheese together by *hand* until blended. Add flour gradually; mix well. Chill several hours or overnight. Roll out dough on board lightly dusted with flour. Cut into 2-in. squares with fluted pastry wheel. Place 1/2 level teaspoon of filling in center of each square. Fold over two corners; pinch to seal. Bake at 350° for about 10-15 minutes. (Cookies will puff up.) Remove to cooling rack. When cool, dust with confectioners' sugar. **Yield:** 6 dozen.

OVERNIGHT DANISH BRAIDS
Judy Amfahr, Ames, Iowa

(PICTURED ON PAGE 88)

- 1 cup butter, room temperature
- 5 cups all-purpose flour
- 1/2 teaspoon salt
- 3 eggs, beaten
- 1 package active dry yeast
- 1/4 cup warm water
- 3/4 cup warm water
- 1/2 cup sugar

FILLING:
- 1 cup butter, softened
- 1 cup brown sugar
- 1 tablespoon cinnamon
- 1 cup chopped pecans

GLAZE:
- 1-1/2 cups confectioners' sugar
- 1 to 2 tablespoons hot milk
- 3 teaspoons melted butter
- 1/2 teaspoon vanilla

Cut butter into flour and salt in large mixing bowl with pastry cutter until mixture resembles cornmeal. Add eggs, yeast dissolved in 1/4 cup water, 3/4 cup water and sugar. Mix by hand until dough is well mixed (batter may be sticky). Refrigerate, covered, for 5-6 hours or overnight. Bring dough to room temperature, about 1 hour. Divide dough into four equal parts. Roll each part into 12- x 9-in. rectangle (like thin cinnamon roll) on floured surface. Prepare filling by combining ingredients until well-mixed. Using 1/2 cup filling per braid, spread in 3-in.-wide strip down center of each rectangle. With kitchen shears, cut sides toward center in strips 3 in. long and 1 in. wide (Fig. 1). (See previous page.) Fold strips over filling, alternating from side to side (Fig. 2). Place on greased cookie sheet; cover and let rise until double. Bake at 350° for 20-25 minutes. Carefully remove to wire rack. Cool slightly. Top with glaze made by mixing ingredients until smooth. **Yield:** 4. (Braids freeze beautifully.)

CHOCOLATE LADIES
Jodie McCoy, Tulsa, Oklahoma

(PICTURED ON PAGE 88)

COOKIE DOUGH:
- 1 cup butter, softened
- 1 package (8 ounces) cream cheese, softened
- 1 cup sugar
- 1/2 teaspoon vanilla
- 2 *tablespoons* grated orange peel
- 2-1/2 cups all-purpose flour
- 1/2 teaspoon salt
- 1-1/4 cups blanched almonds, chopped *very fine,* divided

CHOCOLATE GLAZE:
- 4 ounces semisweet chocolate
- 1/4 cup butter

Cream butter with cream cheese; beat in sugar, vanilla and orange peel until light and fluffy. Mix in flour, salt and *1 cup almonds.* Shape into 1-in. balls. Place on ungreased cookie sheet; flatten with glass dipped in additional sugar. Bake at 325° for 15 minutes. Make glaze by combining chocolate and butter in saucepan. Stir over low heat until melted. Set aside. Transfer baked cookies to wire rack. Spoon 1/2 teaspoon glaze on center of cookie; spread slightly with back of spoon. Sprinkle with remaining almonds. **Yield:** 6 dozen.

FRESH FRUIT WITH ORANGE CHEESE DIP
Vicki Eatwell, Eau Claire, Wisconsin

(PICTURED ON PAGE 88)

DIP:
- 1 package (8 ounces) cream cheese, softened
- 1 cup marshmallow cream

Grated rind from 1 orange

Fresh fruits: pears, apples, grapes, pineapple, melon

Orange or lemon juice

Combine dip ingredients; mix well. Slice washed pears and apples; dip into lemon or orange juice to prevent browning; drain. Pour dip into bowl; place in center of large platter. Arrange fruit around dip.

RHUBARB STRAWBERRY SALAD
Evelyn Sherk, Plattsville, Ontario

(PICTURED ON PAGE 88)

- 4 cups red rhubarb pieces (frozen works fine)
- 2/3 to 3/4 cup sugar
- 2/3 cup water
- 2 boxes (3 ounces *each*) strawberry-flavored gelatin dessert
- 1/2 cup cold water
- 1/2 cup white soda or ginger ale

Grated rind of 1 orange
- 1/3 to 1/2 cup chopped walnuts

Place rhubarb, sugar and water in saucepan. Cook until tender. Strain to remove pulp, if desired. Add gelatin to mixture. Stir well to dissolve. Add water, soda and orange rind. Chill until partially set. Add nuts; mix. Put in oiled fancy ring mold; refrigerate overnight. Unmold on lettuce-lined glass plate. Decorate with unhulled fresh strawberries, if desired. **Yield:** 12 servings.

INDEX